CONTRACT CARPETING

BY LILA SHOSHKES

WHITNEY LIBRARY OF DESIGN,
an imprint of
WATSON-GUPTILL PUBLICATIONS/NEW YORK

First published 1974 in New York by the Whitney Library of Design,
an imprint of Watson-Guptill Publications,
a division of Billboard Publications, Inc.,
One Astor Plaza, New York, N.Y. 10036

Manufactured in U.S.A.

Library of Congress Cataloging in Publication Data
Shoshkes, Lila, 1926–
    Contract carpeting.
    Bibliography: p.
    1. Carpets. I. Title.
TS1775.S47   677'.643   74-13568
ISBN 0-8230-7130-8

First Printing, 1974

Edited by Susan Davis
Designed by James Craig and Bob Fillie
Set in 10 point Vega by Publishers Graphics, Inc.
Printed and bound by Halliday Lithograph Corporation

To Milton

Preface

A carpet specification should be an easy specification to write since carpet has been covering floors for centuries. But contract carpet presents new problems. It is carpet for public spaces, and it is different from carpet for residential use because of its scale, the demands of wear, the safety factors, and the way it is purchased. Because a large part of the total furnishings budget goes to purchase carpet, it is the single largest item to be bought, and it takes the most wear and abuse.

Carpet is newly important as a basic finishing material in the general contract. It is taking the place of traditional flooring materials such as resilient tile or terrazzo. Since the development of long-wearing synthetic fibers, carpet has taken on additional significance because of its economy, ease of maintenance, excellent thermal properties, its acoustical contributions, as well as its positive safety factor. Now carpet is being specified for areas, such as schools and hospitals, where soft covering was never before considered practical. Consequently, the growth of the carpet industry has been tremendous as specifiers and clients have come to realize the good sense of using carpet.

But contract carpeting presents architects, designers, and their clients with enough problems to fill a Pandora's box. Just specifying the best carpet for the particular location leads to the question: How do you know what you want? With that question come all the attendant problems:

What fiber?

What construction?

What padding and installation?

What federal regulations apply?

What standards exist?

How do you control static build-up?

What flammability and smoke standards exist?

How long will it keep its good appearance?

How can you find out? Whom do you believe?

Traditionally, architects, designers, and institutional or corporate purchasers turn to mill representatives and experienced dealers as sources of information. Although they are knowledgeable, the fact remains that the impartial specifier needs impartial information. There are a few consultants available, but too often they have commercial interests.

Designers, architects, and others who specify have accumulated valuable knowledge through long experience, but they have been busy pursuing their active careers and have not been able to share their knowledge with others in the field. Specifiers who try to inform themselves have found a confusing array of conflicting information matched by a vast amount of technical data. Frequently, the information is not available in usable form or is difficult to correlate with real situations. The Carpet and Rug Institute generously offers a wealth of technical assistance and information but reflects and protects the interests of the industry that it represents.

A study of contract carpeting that I made while at the interior design firm of ISD showed me how little practical information designers have to work with. I wrote this book to provide realistic observations based on actual performance and to bring together in one source all the available information.

I did not intend this work as a "how to do it" book for specifiers. Rather, I hope this book will be a first step in establishing a body of knowledge from which realistic standards may evolve. Also, I hope it will initiate a dialogue among professionals involved with manufacturing, specifying, and using contract carpet.

This study is solely concerned with modern, commercial, machine-made products. It does not include such interesting carpets as Rya, braided, embroidered, or hooked or Navajo, Persian, Chinese, Indian, Turkish, and Moroccan rugs. These beautiful floor coverings are used in contract work as accents and luxurious area rugs and are selected for their individual quality and design.

The information gathered here comes from many sources. Bringing it all together has been a stimulating challenge. To the collected data, I have added my own experiences as an interior designer, my observations of carpeting installations, and information gathered from conversations with many people.

My grateful thanks are due to all who have assisted me in preparing the material in this book by providing encouragement, information, and their personal experience. I have talked to maintenance men, mill representatives, salesmen, dealers, installers, public relations people, purchasing agents, business managers, bankers, government representatives, school principals, university administrators, museum directors, hospital administrators, safety engineers, architects, designers, fiber producers, industry representatives. And I visited the Lee's carpet mill in Glasgow, Virginia. I would like to thank them all.

Among the industry representatives who have assisted me, I would like to thank the following for generously supplying technical materials and photographs: Alden Carpet Company, Allied Chemical Company, The American Hotel and Motel Association, Armstrong Carpets, Bigelow Carpets, Brunswick Corporation, The Carpet and Rug Institute, Dow-Badische, DuPont Company, The General Services Administration, Hercules Incorporated, The Jute Carpet Backing Council, Lee's Carpets (Burlington Industries), Mohawk Carpets (Mohasco), Monsanto Textile Company, The Olin Corporation, The Ozite Corporation, and The Wool Bureau.

Of the many individuals who encouraged me and were so giving in their cooperation to make this book possible, I would like to thank Olga Gueft for her initial understanding and swift support, Milton Schottenfeld for his kind and authoritative review and advice, Jeanne Weeks for her clarifying comments, and Susan Davis for bringing order and logic to this work.

Contents

Introduction: A History of Woven Floor Coverings

Carpeting has been part of the development of civilizations in most parts of the world. The relative skills and artistic development of a culture are reflected in its rug making, whether in the rugs of the Navaho Indians, the fabled carpets of Persia, or the products of the modern carpet industry that developed as a result of the Industrial Revolution.

The earliest humans eased their feet and softened their hearth with sand, grasses, pine boughs, and animal skins. During the Paleolithic times there are records of plaited rushes used as floor coverings. The earliest existing fragment of a floor covering is one of felt, made in the 4th century B.C. and found in a mountain cave in Turkistan. Legends handed down through the years refer to the fabulous rugs of the Assyrian and Babylonian civilizations that existed between 3000 and 546 B.C. After the Persian king Cyrus defeated Croesus of Lydia, the Persians acquired the art of rug making. Records indicate that their rugs were thick, resilient, and enriched with gold.

Flat-woven and knotted-pile carpets became a major art form of the Middle Eastern countries. The rise of Islam in the 6th century A.D. encouraged the art of rug making, which ranged from the widely used prayer rugs and tent adornments to the fabulous palace carpets. The nomadic shepards were rug makers and traders who introduced Persian rugs to China as early as the 6th and 7th centuries. The Persian court rugs of that period were made by trained

Figure 1. Weaving in Europe about 1300. Flat woven tapestry carpets like Aubussons and Gobelins were woven on these high-warp looms. Courtesy New York Public Library.

weavers who faithfully copied the cartoons drawn by great Persian miniaturists in cashmere, angora, camel hair, and sheep's wool, and woven with silk and gold threads. The art of rug making developed to such a point that rugs became a symbol of wealth and ornament and were valued by oriental potentates and great nobility. This art reached a peak of perfection from the 15th to 17th centuries. As the Moslem world expanded westward and as Europeans came into contact with the Moslem culture during the Crusades, these rugs were introduced into Europe.

Europeans had been producing flat-weave tapestries to adorn castle walls since about 1000 A.D. Flemish, Gobelin, and Aubusson tapestries became famous (Fig. 1). Since the work of producing tapestries and carpets was slow and required great skill, they were extremely expensive.

The knotted-pile carpets that reached Europe from the Middle East were made for the courts of kings. They were highly prized and were considered part of the royal treasuries. The first governmental support for carpet weaving came in 1605, when Henry IV of France established workrooms to produce so-called Oriental rugs. These workrooms were soon moved out to an abandoned building that had been a soap factory, and the rugs became known as "Savonnerie" from the French word for soap—*savon* (Fig. 2). That name has since become synonymous with pile carpets of fine velvety quality.

Figure 2. *Making a Savonnerie rug, with the tools used shown below. Pierre Dupont developed a method of weaving pile fabrics and presented Henry IV of France with an essay about it. He won royal support in 1605 to develop what have become known as Savonnerie rugs. Courtesy New York Public Library.*

England's royalty had very few carpets even during the 17th century. We know that Henry VIII had Turkish carpets because they appear in the paintings of Hans Holbein. But they must have been scarce since both Henry and his daughter, Elizabeth I, ordered fresh rushes to be laid every day in the great halls. When Elizabeth ordered carpets laid, they were placed over three layers of sweet rushes, and it was noted as a memorable occasion.

Louis XIV of France (Fig. 3) inadvertently contributed to the development of the carpet industry in England, and its partial collapse in France, when he revoked the Edict of Nantes in 1695. Since religious protection for Protestants was no longer guaranteed, many Protestant weavers fled from France. Some settled in Belgium and copied Orientals, which became known as "Brussels" carpets. Other immigrating French weavers found safety in England, where they set up small rug-making establishments that produced hand-loomed carpets in Axminster and Wilton. A larger-scaled carpet-knotting industry began in the middle of the 18th century in Axminster, and mechanized rug looms were introduced in Wilton in 1740 (Fig. 4). England's fine carpets were in great demand in colonial America. George Washington wrote to England in 1797 to order Wilton carpeting for the refurbishing of Mount Vernon.

England provided the right combination of circumstances that initiated the Industrial Revolution and

Figure 3. (Left) One of a series of 90 rugs woven for Louis XIV, about 1672, for use in the Louvre. Courtesy New York Public Library.

Figure 4. (Right) A carpet weaving workroom in England about 1750, where French techniques were used by workmen who had emigrated from France. Courtesy New York Public Library.

A

B

C

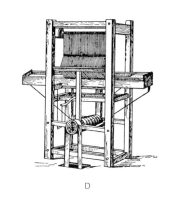

D

Figure 5. *The start of the Industrial Revolution began with these simple inventions: the spinning wheel (A) gives way to the spinning jenny (B), and the hand loom (C) is supplanted by the first power loom (D). Courtesy New York Public Library.*

transformed the textile industry. Only minor changes were necessary to convert manufacturing processes from hand operation to semi-automatic or automatic operation using mechanical power. The first great invention was the flying shuttle in 1733. It was followed by the spinning jenny in 1764, the power loom in 1785 (Fig. 5), and the Jacquard attachment in 1800 (Fig. 6).

New inventions spurred industrialization, but the following factors also contributed:

1. Capital for investment was readily available and at low interest rates.

2. A good labor supply was available because serfdom and the guild system had almost disappeared in England.

3. There was a readily available supply of iron for machinery and coal for power.

4. The factory system as a way of organizing production and labor, which was developed at the Gobelin carpet works in France, was put into practice in England at Wilton.

5. England's growing colonies provided an expanding market for her products.

Further industrialization of carpet making occurred in the United States after the American Revolution. The first carpet factory was started in Philadelphia in 1791. The basic weaves were established and named for the towns in England where they originated, and in 1791

the first Axminster was made in Quakerstown, Pennsylvania. The first power loom for weaving rugs was invented by Erastus Bigelow of Lowell, Massachusetts, in 1839 and perfected in 1848 (Fig. 7). John Johnson· of Halifax, England, produced pattern carpets of velvet and tapestry weaves in Newark, New Jersey, in the 1850s by printing color on the yarns. The mechanical Axminster weave was developed in 1876 and perfected by Alexander Smith using the spool developed by Skinner in 1867. In 1878 the Shuttleworth family established a factory in Amsterdam, New York, that had 14 Wilton looms with Jacquard attachments brought from England. These first looms were operated by water power.

Until the 19th century the word "carpet" was used to describe any cover made of thick material. Now it is used to mean a large-size soft floor covering.

The first machine-made carpeting was only 27 inches wide because of the narrow looms that had to be used. After the early 1900s, loom width became enlarged. By 1935 the word "broadloom" was a generally accepted term for all wide-width woven carpets. Today widths of carpeting of 9, 12, 15, and 18 feet, as well as 27 and 54 inches, can be produced.

The major contribution to carpet manufacturing in the 20th century was the development of the tufting process. It was based on a handicraft activity of colonial housewives

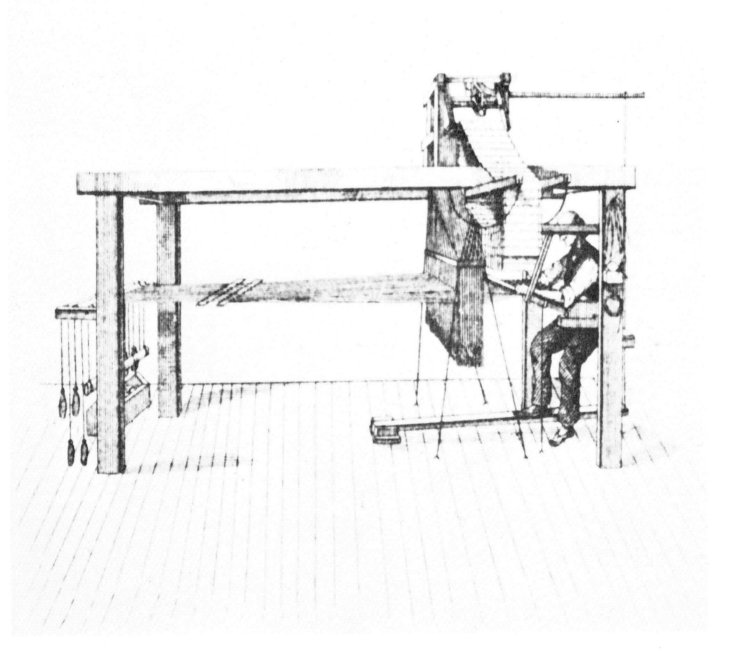

Figure 6. An early Jacquard loom used in the 1800s.
This invention completely revolutionized the production of figured weaving.
Courtesy New York Public Library.

known as "candle wicking," or the hand tufting of cotton bedspreads. In 1900 Catherine Evans perfected a method of locking a tuft of yarn into a fabric backing by having the fabric shrink around the tuft. Soon she was selling so many bedspreads that she contracted work throughout the local community of Dalton, Georgia. As a result of minimum wage legislation in 1937, the handicraft industry changed. Expensive hand labor was replaced with newly developed tufting machines.

In 1948 the first broadloom tufted carpets were produced in Dalton, utilizing the principles of making tufted bedspreads and rugs. Today tufted carpets account for over 90 percent of the carpets made, replacing woven carpets because of the speed, efficiency, and economy of the tufting process.

Figure 7. By 1862 weaving power-loomed pile carpets was a growing industry. Courtesy New York Public Library.

PART I

CARPET
CONSTRUCTION
SPECIFICATIONS

The Components
of a
Specification

There are two important kinds of carpet—woven carpets and tufted carpets—that are defined according to their method of construction. Woven carpets are made by constructing the face pile and the backing simultaneously to create an integral product. Woven carpets can be made on three different types of looms, each resulting in a different type of carpet: Axminsters, Wiltons, or velvets. Tufted carpets are made by a series of needles that stitch each loop or tuft into a separate backing fabric. Most carpets today are tufted because they are more economical to produce. These two methods of construction, by which the majority of carpets are made today, will be discussed in greater detail in Chapter 2.

Woven and tufted carpets have similar specifications and their specifications can be compared. Each element in their specification represents a technical aspect that affects performance. Performance can be defined as a function of the elements of a specification. It includes wearability, abrasion resistance, resilience, crush resistance, texture retention, resistance to soiling, cleanability, static control, color retention, flame resistance, and sound absorption.

Construction specifications are selected in relation to the traffic the carpet will receive. The Canadian Government Specifications Board, in their bulletin "Standards for Commercial Carpet" (4-GP-129), and the American Hotel and Motel Association have classified areas according to the amount of expected foot traffic. Areas that can be expected to have heavy foot traffic are

Entrance ways and lobbies

Stairways and elevators

Aisles and corridors

Reception areas

Open work areas

Dining areas, bars, and grills

Public rooms and wards

Let us examine the elements of carpet construction (Fig. 8) and see how they affect performance.

Pitch, Gauge, and Needles per Inch

Pitch, gauge, and needles per inch are equivalents. Pitch is a unit of measure used to describe woven carpets, and gauge or needles per inch are used to describe tufted carpets.

Pitch is the number of loops of yarn in 27 inches across the width of the loom. It indicates the closeness of the weave crosswise. A "216 pitch" means that 216 lines of yarn run through each 27 inches on the loom.

Gauge is comparable with pitch in tufted carpet construction. Gauge is the spacing between needles across the width of the loom, and it is expressed in fractions of an inch.

Needles per Inch is the number of tufting needles per inch across the

loom, which indicates the closeness of the weave, as does pitch.

Pitch, gauge, and needles per inch, if taken together, are one of the factors which determine carpet *density*. A higher pitch denotes a closer weave. The higher the number of needles per inch in tufting, the greater the possibility that the backing fabric might suffer. The weave will be closer but the dimensional stability will be weaker than that of the comparable woven carpet.

Rows per Inch and Stitches per Inch

Rows per inch and stitches per inch are also equivalents.

Rows per Inch is the number of wires or loops per inch along the selvage length of a woven carpet. The term "wire" refers to the metal strip in the loom that is inserted in the yarn to form a uniform loop of a specific height in a woven carpet.

Stitches per Inch is the number of stitches a tufting needle takes lengthwise per inch.

Tufts per Square Inch

The combination of the number of stitches or loops across the loom with the number of stitches or loops down the fabric is the number of *tufts per square inch*. This is a most significant measurement and a true indicator of density of construction, which affects quality and performance. Density of construction is one of the primary factors in the amount

of wear that a carpet can be expected to take. The greater the traffic, the higher the density of the carpet required for the area.

When yarns are tightly packed together, they give each other support; this applies to all fibers. Greater density increases the support of the tufts and results in better performance. Soiling does not penetrate the carpet, but remains on the surface, which makes for easier cleaning, and there is greater resiliency, crush resistance, and texture retention.

Tufts per square inch can be calculated by multiplying the number of tufts down per inch by the number of tufts across per inch. For example, 216 pitch is 8 needles, or 8 loops of yarn, per inch across the loom, multiplied by (let's take a typical condition) 8 rows per inch along the length. That equals 64 tufts per square inch.

Table 1 can be used to compare and evaluate carpet specifications. It indicates:

1. The relationships among the different elements of pitch, needles, gauge, and rows or stitches.

2. The number of tufts per square inch of the most commonly used carpet constructions.

Look at Table 1 to see the range of construction of the following carpets:

1. *Shags* range from 108 to 180 pitch and have low density and few tufts per square inch. These characteristics are offset by high piles and heavier yarns.

Figure 8. *The elements of carpet construction.*
Courtesy Bigelow Carpet Co.

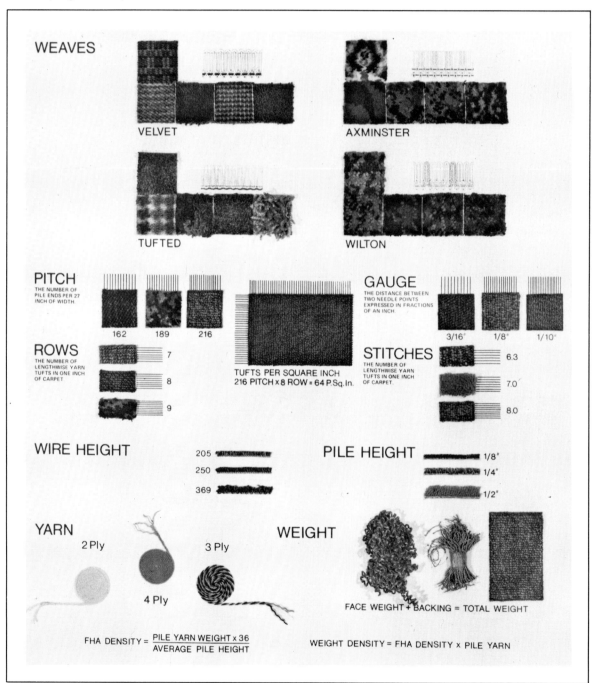

TABLE 1. Tufts per Square Inch*

Common Carpet Constructions

Pitch	108	143.9	172.8	180	189	216	243	252	256	270	346
Needles	4	5.3	6.4	6.6	7	8	9	9.3	9.5	10	12.8
Gauge	1/4	3/16	5/32		9/64	1/8	1/9			1/10	5/64
Rows or Stitches per Inch:											
5	20	26.5	32	33	35	40	45	46.5	47.5	50	64
6	24	31.8	38.4	39.6	42	48	54	55.8	57	60	73.2
7	28	34.1	44.8	46.2	49	56	63	65.1	66.5	70	89.6
8	32	42.4	51.2	52.8	56	64	72	74.4	76	80	102.4
9	36	47.7	57.2	59.4	63	72	81	83.7	85.5	90	115.2
10	40	53	64	66	70	80	90	93	95	100	128
11	44	58.3	70.4	72.6	77	88	99	102.3	104.5	110	140.8

*Number of tufts per square inch is determined by multiplying needles corresponding to a particular pitch or gauge by rows or stitches per inch. For example, for 243 pitch, 9 needles times 10 stitches per inch equals 90 tufts per square inch.

TABLE 2. Comparison of Two Carpet Specifications

Carpet	Construction	Pitch/Gauge	Row/Stitch	Tufts, PSI	Face Weight	Pile Height
A	Tufted	1/10	7	70	48	.218
B	Velvet	216	8	64	48	.312

Level-loop pile. Level loops form the carpet surface. Low, level-loop construction is frequently selected for heavy-duty wear. The texture wears well, but shows dirt and lint readily. Patterns of alternating cut and uncut level loops make a handsome variation.

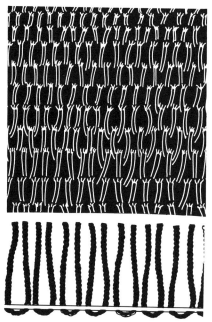

Cut pile. A low, cut pile is a plush; the higher piles range from splush to shag. Low, dense plushes stand upright and form an even surface that is subject to shading. Shading is the illusion of color change that is caused by bent yarns reflecting light in different directions, giving tonal highlights.

Level tip shear. This cut and loop construction can have a random pattern as shown or a grid effect. The sheared design will show shading where it is cut.

Random shear. This texture is similar to a multilevel loop except that the highest level of loop is cut. Tremendous pattern effects are possible. The sheared portions appear darker and heighten the dimensional effect.

Frieze or twist. Yarns are tightly twisted and heat set to increase resilience and durability. Carpets of frieze or twist design wear well and are not difficult to vacuum if they have a level surface.

Shags. Pile yarn from 1 1/2 to 3 inches or more in length that is either looped or cut and has a tumbled, random appearance. A twist is heat set into the yarn to reduce shedding. Shags wear on the sides of the yarn. They hide footprints and conceal soiling very effectively, but are difficult to vacuum.

Multilevel loop. Pile yarns are looped at several levels. This texture hides footprints, dirt, and dust better than a level loop, but it shows crushing and compression with wear.

Sculptured or carved. The pile yarns are sheared at different levels to make a textured design. Sculptured or carved designs are not generally used for contract work because they show crushing and compression with wear.

Figure 9. *Textures. Courtesy Armstrong Cork Co.*

2. *Axminsters* range from 180 to 216 pitch and 8 to 11 rows. Medium grades have from 42 to 49 tufts per square inch. Heavier grades have over 52 tufts per square inch.

3. *Wiltons* range from 180 to 256 pitch and from 6 to 10 wires or rows. Heavier grades have over 52 tufts per square inch.

4. *Velvets* range from 162 to 270 pitch and from 6 to 10 wires or rows. Heavier grades have over 64 tufts per square inch.

5. *Tufteds* range from 4 to 12 needles per inch and from 5 to 10 stitches per inch. Heavier grades have over 64 tufts per square inch.

To show how Table 1 can be used, let us compare the tufts per square inch of two typical carpets and determine which carpet is most densely constructed and which, therefore, will give better wear. If the face weights (defined below) are equal, the carpet with more tufts per square inch will outwear the other.

In Table 2, we see that carpet A, a tufted carpet, has more tufts per square inch, making it the tighter, denser carpet. Therefore, it will show less pile crush and will not show wear as quickly. If we look for a softer carpet for an area that does not receive the heaviest traffic, carpet B, a velvet carpet with fewer tufts and a higher pile height, will be softer to walk on—relatively more luxurious underfoot. Both carpets A and B have been labeled by the manufacturer as suitable for heavy traffic areas, but we can see that car-

pet A is better suited to such areas than carpet B.

Face Weight

The *face weight* of the carpet yarn is measured in ounces per square yard. It is the amount of yarn used in the pile of the carpet, excluding the backing. Face weights of wool can be compared with those of acrylics and polyesters, and face weights of nylon can be compared with those of polypropylene. *Face weight is a good indicator of service quality.*

Let us summarize what we've discussed thus far: *The architect or designer can evaluate carpet specifications by comparing tufts per square inch and face weights and relating them to established minimum standards for quality and traffic.*

Pile Height

Pile height is an important component in carpet specification (Fig. 9).

Pile Height is the height of the loop or tuft measured in decimals of an inch from the backing to the top of the carpet. It can also be called *wire height* since in woven carpets the yarn is looped over a metal strip or wire of a given height to make the loop. Here are several characteristics of pile height:

1. A low, level loop performs best for heavy-duty wear.

2. A high pile gives a feeling of luxury.

3. Pile height is one of the determining factors in areas where the pile has crushed.

4. Carpets with low, dense pile will crush less than those having higher piles.

5. Pile heights frequently vary in carpets with textured surfaces (but textured surfaces are not always created by multilevel piles).

6. Single-level pile will wear better than multilevel pile. Wear on multilevel pile tends to bend and crush the higher pile until it is worn to the height of the lower pile.

A guide for the minimum face weights and pile heights in relation to traffic wear has been suggested by the American Hotel and Motel Association. For average heavy foot traffic areas, 42 ounces *minimum* weight per square yard is recommended for wool or acrylic carpet, or 28 ounces for nylon or polypropylene (olefin). For average medium foot traffic, 36 ounces *minimum* weight per square yard is recommended for wool or acrylic carpet, or 22 ounces for nylon or polyprolypene (see Tables E and F in the Appendix).

Fiber

Fiber is important to carpet performance. It affects wearability, abrasion resistance, resilience, texture retention, resistance to boiling, static build-up, and flame resistance. With so much demanded of a fiber, it is understandable that no one fiber can satisfy all demands equally well. Carpet fibers will be discussed at length in Chapter 3.

In a carpet specification the fiber used must be identified by its generic name. In the case of blends, each fiber must be identified in order of its predominance in the fabric. These requirements are specified by the Textile Products Identification Act of the Federal Trade Commission. The fiber's trade name will probably be used in addition to its generic name because the trade name represents technological refinements over the basic forms of the fiber identified generically. Trade names are important because there are differences between nylons, for example, of the same generic family. A list of the major fiber producers and their trade names is given in Table D in the Appendix.

The development of synthetic fibers has been progressing under pressure of fierce competition among fiber producers and demand for better fibers from the end user. Fiber producers now realize their involvement extends beyond the production stages. They are now developing carpet specifications that utilize fibers that give maximum performance. DuPont, Monsanto, Beaunit, Hercules, and Allied Chemical are actively concerned with the end products' performance.

Man-made fiber production for carpet yarns takes two forms: filament yarns from continuous monofilaments and staple yarns from staple fibers (Fig. 10).

Filament Yarns are made of two or more monofilaments (a monofilament is a single continuous fiber strand) assembled or held together by twisting. Added physical properties can be achieved by heat setting or twisting and untwisting, crimping, knitting, and deknitting. The bulk or stretch properties that are added to filament yarns this way add dimension and texture, and such filaments are sometimes referred to as bulked continuous filaments (BCF).

Staple Yarns are spun, and the short ends of fiber are twisted into yarn. Yarns that are spun are more irregular than filament yarns, and they are bulkier than filament yarns of the same weight.

Longer staple fibers are spun into worsted yarns. The fibers are corded and combed so that only the longer fibers are used, and they are laid as parallel as possible before spinning. These yarns are used for cut pile, in which the yarn stands more erect and does not shed.

Wool, acrylics, and polyesters are available only as staple yarns. Nylons and polypropylenes are available as both staple and filament yarns. Blends of fibers such as wool and nylon are made of staple fibers, blended before the yarn is spun. Staple yarns characteristically shed when new, and the short fiber ends collect on the surface of the pile. With many synthetics, the loose fibers become entangled and form a ball, which is called *pilling*. Such synthetic fibers tend to hold fast be-

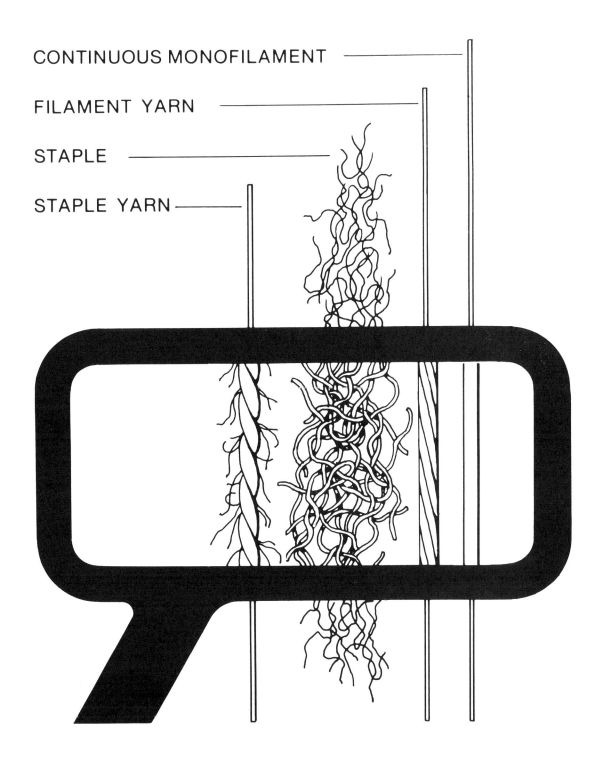

Figure 10. Forms of man-made fibers.
Courtesy Man-Made Fiber
Producers Association, Inc.

CONTINUOUS MONOFILAMENT

FILAMENT YARN

STAPLE

STAPLE YARN

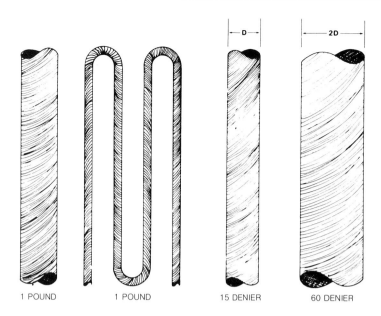

1 POUND   1 POUND   15 DENIER   60 DENIER

Figure 11. Yarn count. Carpet fibers are measured by yarn length and weight. A length of yarn that weighs 1 pound is called a hank. One hank is equal to 840 lineal yards weighing 1 pound. The number of hanks needed to weigh 1 pound determines the count. The larger the count, the finer the yarn. Courtesy Armstrong Cork Co.

Figure 12. Denier. The denier system originated centuries ago in France where the weight of a particular length of yarn was measured by the weight of copper coins known as deniers. Today denier is the weight in grams of 9,000 meters of yarn. The lower the denier, the finer the yarns. Courtesy Armstrong Cork Co.

Figure 13. Ply. Yarns are plied to make them thicker, bulkier, and have more body. Single strands of yarn are twisted together to form one yarn end; for example, two-ply yarn is two strands of yarn twisted together. Courtesy Armstrong Cork Co.

cause of the tensile strength of the fiber, but foot traffic does wear them away in time.

Single strands of yarn are spun to a specific weight. The weight or thickness of a strand of yarn gives the yarn its unique characteristics. The weight of a single strand of yarn is not readily available, but it reflects itself in the face weight of the carpet. Weight is expressed two ways: as yarn count or denier.

Yarn Count is the actual number of yards per ounce of yarn. For example, 1/110 means one-ply of yarn extends 110 lineal yards per ounce. The same yarn in two-ply is expressed as 2/55; that is, two plys of yarn extend 55 yards per ounce. As a three-ply, it is expressed as 3/37. The lower the number of yards per ounce, the heavier the yarn (Fig. 11).

Denier is the weight of yarn in grams per 9,000 meters. One denier equals 4,464,528 yards per pound, or 279,033 yards per ounce. To find the yards per ounce, divide 279,033 by the denier number. The lower the denier, the finer the filament of yarn. Nylon and polypropylene deniers are typically .2500 and .3000. Most mills use a variety of yarn weights in their products for different textures and prices (Fig. 12).

Ply is the number of strands of single yarns twisted together to form one carpet yarn. It can vary from one- to six-ply depending on the texture wanted. Ply is not a measure of quality; yarn weight is more significant (Fig. 13).

When a yarn contains more than one color, it is called a *moresque yarn*. Moresque yarns are used to produce tweeds.

Color

Color is the designer's province. Color choice is unlimited, however esthetic decisions can be affected by the following observations:

1. Nothing else has the impact of color in the appearance of carpeting.

2. The floor is the largest color area of the interior being designed.

3. Color is affected by the quality of light that it receives—sunlight, incandescent light, or fluorescent light—the type of soil in the area, and the amount of traffic the carpet receives.

4. Extremes of color magnify soiling.

5. Yellow colors show more soiling.

6. Patterns and mixtures with white show more soiling than those without white, but patterns and mixtures of any color including white show less soil than most solid colors.

7. Solid colors show more footprints, dirt, and lint.

8. Carpets of natural wool show the least soil and wear better than dyed wool fibers.

9. Color can be used to conceal cigarette burns and soiling.

Colorfastness is a function of filament structure and dye selection. Depending on the type of dye that is used, colorfastness can vary even in the same fiber produced by different manufacturers. The architect and designer can protect themselves by requiring that the carpet meet established standards of fading, colorfastness, and imperviousness to carpet cleaning solutions. The carpet manufacturer has the responsibility of meeting these standards according to test methods established by the American Association of Textile Chemists and Colorists (AATCC). See Table 3.

TABLE 3. PERFORMANCE TESTS FOR COLORFASTNESS

Performance Test	Test Method	Minimum Acceptable Result*
Colorfastness to crocking (wet or dry)	AATCC 8	4
Colorfastness to light	AATCC 16-E	Light colors stable for 40 hours; dark colors, 80 hours
Colorfastness to water	AATCC 107	3.5
Colorfastness to ozone	AATCC 109	4
Colorfastness to ozone in high humidity areas	AATCC 129	4

*These tests measure results according to a range from 5 to 1, where 5 represents negligible or no color change or excellent resistance to change.

Dyeing and Printing

Fibers can be dyed at three different stages in carpet manufacture: before spinning, after spinning, and after weaving.

Dyeing before Spinning can be done by either of two processes: stock dyeing or solution dyeing.

Stock Dyeing. Blended wool is dyed prior to becoming yarn. It can be dyed in small batches and blended to a uniform color. The color is dependable even in large orders. Most mills stock between 50 and 100 colors for special orders.

Solution Dyeing. Dye stuffs are added to the liquid chemical compounds that will be spun into fibers, becoming an integral part of the fiber. The dye permeates the entire fiber and is long lasting and resistant to fading and crocking.

Dyeing after Spinning can be done by one of three processes: skein dyeing, package dyeing, or space dyeing.

Skein Dyeing. Blended yarns are spun into skeins, which are stored and dyed as orders are obtained. Such skeins can be dyed any desired color in limited amounts. The colors are usually clearer than those produced by stock dyeing.

Package Dyeing. This method is not unlike skein dyeing, except that the fibers are wound on perforated packages, and the dye stuff is forced under pressure from inside the package through the yarn. Unlimited color is available.

Space Dyeing. Yarn is treated with three or more colors so that the carpet pile is given a random pattern. Sometimes a chevron effect occurs when a large area covered with this carpeting is viewed from a distance—the pattern seems to blend into an overall irregular zigzag design.

After Weaving either piece dyeing or printing are the coloring methods used. After dyeing, the carpets are washed and dried and the backings are applied.

Piece Dyeing. This dyeing procedure is generally associated with tufted nylon carpets. Piece dyeing can be done in small batches of 300 to 700 yards or as a continuous operation with the *Kuster* method of applying a solid film of dye (Fig. 14). A *TAK* attachment can then be used to add a random dot or patterned effect by spattering the carpet with one or two additional colors (Figs. 15 and 16). This method makes it possible for the mills to stockpile undyed carpets, since they are dyed as orders are received and costly inventories are minimized.

A piece-dyed carpet can also be *cross* dyed (cross dyeing is also known as *differential* dyeing). Cross dyeing uses fibers treated to accept or reject certain dyes. Carpets tufted with a combination of such yarns can look, when dyed, like a tweed or have a moresque effect from a single dye bath.

Figure 14. Carpet after dyeing in a Kuster range. Courtesy Du Pont Magazine.

Figure 15. *TAK machine spatters newly dyed carpet with one or two additional colors for a random dot effect. Courtesy Du Pont Magazine.*

Figure 16. Carpet with TAK effect.
Courtesy Du Pont Magazine.

Figure 18. *The printing element in the Stalwart printer is composed of soft sponge rubber glued to a neoprene rubber base that is tacked to a wooden roller. Courtesy Monsanto.*

Figure 17. *Diagram of a Stalwart machine printing with three colors. If a background color is required, it is generally applied in a prior step and overprinted in the Stalwart. Courtesy Monsanto.*

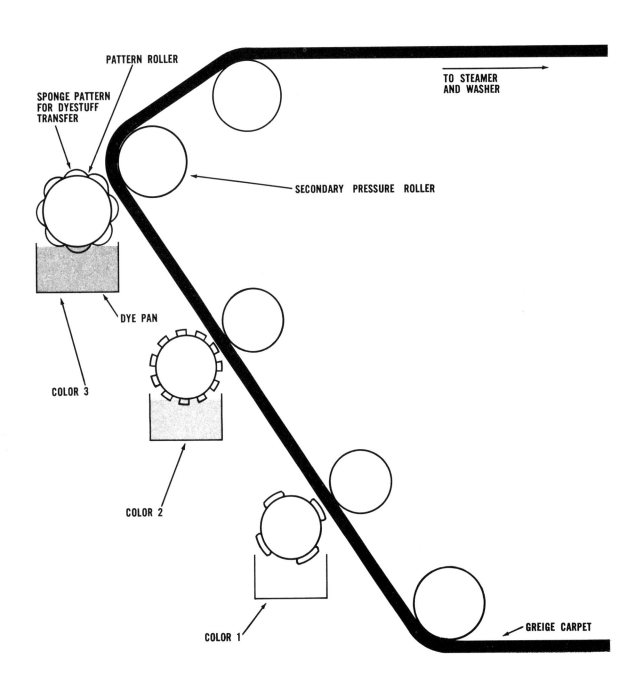

PATTERN ROLLER

SPONGE PATTERN
FOR DYESTUFF
TRANSFER

TO STEAMER
AND WASHER

SECONDARY PRESSURE ROLLER

DYE PAN

COLOR 3

COLOR 2

COLOR 1

GREIGE CARPET

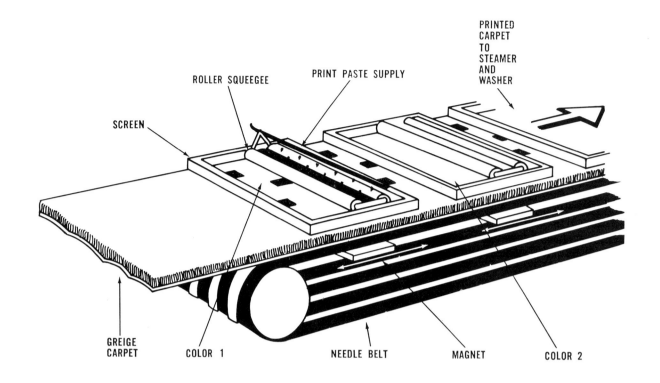

SCREEN ROLLER SQUEEGEE PRINT PASTE SUPPLY PRINTED CARPET TO STEAMER AND WASHER

GREIGE CARPET COLOR 1 NEEDLE BELT MAGNET COLOR 2

Figure 19. Diagram of the flat bed Zimmer printing machine. The Zimmer has excellent register, although a common technique is to lay down a heavy, dark shade over the boundaries of the other colors to ease manufacturing precision and the positioning of other screens. Courtesy Monsanto.

Figure 20. Flat bed Zimmer printer showing actual printing screen. Courtesy E. T. Barwick Industries, Inc.

Piece dyeing can be done in limited batches in a dye beck (stainless steel tank) or in large continuous ranges. Limited quantities mean that color matching must be done within that dye lot. Continuous dyeing presents problems with side matching, which become evident when the carpets are installed. When carpets are seamed side by side and the color does not match or patterns do not line up, it could be the result of uneven color application, tension, or stretching as the carpet travels through the piece-dyeing operation.

Carpet Printing. Print dyeing allows totally uncolored carpets to be styled with an unlimited range of colorful designs. Any pattern can be printed directly on the pile using silk screen techniques. Carpet printing copies the look of Axminsters, Wiltons, Orientals, or any other pattern, but at a much lower cost. (The looms that traditionally produce these patterns are disappearing from the mills as the economics of the industry force manufacturers to search for faster and cheaper means of producing patterns.)

Printing equipment is being developed in Europe and America. Deep color penetration of the pile has been perfected using electrostatic charges that force premetalized dyes into the pile.

There are two basic methods of printing—roller printing and screen printing. *Roller printing* as done by the Stalwart machine is also called *drum printing.* The drum contains the dye that is squeezed through the pattern attachment and printed on the carpet that is on a moving belt (Figs. 17 and 18). *Screen printing* is done on the Zimmer printer, which is a flatbed printing machine. Dye paste is forced through the screens by an electromagnetic system that controls the squeegees, and the machine can print up to six colors simultaneously (Figs. 19 and 20).

With both printing methods, pattern registration is good, but some problems exist. For example, matching patterns over two or three widths can be difficult as variations often develop in the printing. If the repeat of a pattern is 18 inches, sometimes the slippage at the end of one roll can be 19 or 20 inches. When such rolls are lined up side by side, the patterns will not match.

Pattern alignment technology will undoubtedly be improved as printing methods are perfected.

Methods of Construction

Carpeting is classified by the method used to construct it. In this chapter woven, tufted, needlebonded, knitted, and loomed carpets are described.

Woven Carpets

Woven carpets are velvets, Wiltons, and Axminsters. They are created by an interlocking weaving of the surface yarns and the backing materials. As a result they are the most dimensionally stable carpets and have the best wearing qualities of all methods of construction. They are ideal for heavy traffic areas.

Velvets. Velvets are widely used in heavy commercial areas where a strong pattern is not required. For instance, they are found in schools, hospitals, banks, and offices.

The pile surface is formed as the loom loops the warp strands over raised wire stripes that are inserted across the loom. As each row of loops is completed, the wire is withdrawn. The height of the wire determines the height of the pile. Cut pile is made by placing a cutting edge on the end of the wire that cuts the loop as it is removed. Random shearing is also used to vary surface effects (Fig. 21).

For the greatest strength and wearability, velvets should be made with the yarn woven through the back in an all-loop pile. An additional benefit of doing this is that each individual tuft is locked in place. After a woven-through-the-back velvet is finished, it may be cut in any direction without unraveling. This assures excellent seams, as well as ease in patching. This advantage is lost to a slight extent in all-loop pile, double-heddle velvets where the staggered rows of loops do not line up for a straight seam.

Design Considerations. Velvets are limited in design to solid colors and variations of stripes and checks. The velvet loom's lack of ability to make patterns is limiting, but the variations possible within the capabilities of the loom allow for a rich vocabulary. Solid colors can be worked with many textural variations, such as multilevel pile heights and cut and uncut patterns, as well as the traditional round wire pile. Variations can be enriched with moresque yarns (two or more strands of different colors) and double-heddle modifications.

Specifications. A high-quality velvet has from 8 to 10 wires or rows per inch and a pitch of 216 to 279 per 27-inch width, or 64 to 100 tufts per square inch. A medium-quality velvet has 7 to 9 wires per square inch with a pitch of 189 to 243 per 27-inch width, or 49 to 81 tufts per square inch. The lowest-quality velvets have from 6 to 7 wires per inch and a pitch of 162 to 189 per 27-inch width, or 43 to 49 tufts per square inch.

High-speed velvet looms are far more efficient than Wiltons, but less efficient than tufting looms. One compensation is that small runs can be made in special colors. For a run of a special color to be efficient, it should be 500 square yards or more.

Wiltons. The Wilton loom operates on the same basic principle as the velvet loom, but it has the added versatility of the Jacquard attachment. The Jacquard mechanism enables it to produce patterned carpets of almost unlimited designs with up to six colors. The Jacquard mechanism uses punched cards, similar to a player piano roll, to control the selection of yarns from creels to form the pattern. The cards match the entire surface design of the carpet.

Each color used in a pattern is called a *frame.* As the loom operates, the cards indicate which frame will be lifted to the surface and which will be buried in the body. As one color at a time is being drawn through the pile, the others remain beneath the surface (Fig. 22). The addition of each frame adds to the weight of the carpet, but not the pile yarn, as the yarns are buried in the backing. This results in added strength and resilience, and is sometimes referred to as Wilton's hidden value, but the pile surface still must take the wear.

The surface loops are formed over wires, the same as velvets, and can be cut or uncut. Brussels is the old name for uncut Wiltons.

Design Considerations. Wilton carpet construction is the sturdiest carpet weave, and that is why Wiltons are used for the heaviest commercial traffic areas. The pattern capabilities of the Wilton loom give this weave great design flexibility since almost any design can be produced. Pile heights can be varied and the surface can be cut or uncut. The

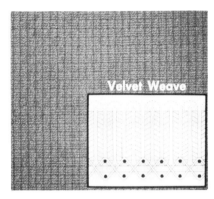

Figure 21. *Velvet weave. Courtesy Du Pont Co.*

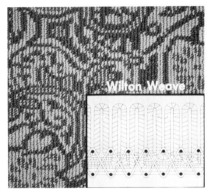

Figure 22. *Wilton weave. Courtesy Du Pont Co.*

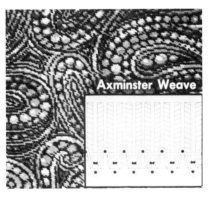

Figure 23. *Axminster weave. Courtesy Du Pont Co.*

slowness of the weave because of the complicated pattern attachments and the amount of required yarn that is not on the carpet face make the price of Wiltons exceed all other weaves.

Wilton carpets are used in theaters and restaurants, where a combination of wearability and aesthetics surpasses all other requirements in importance.

Specifications. A high-quality Wilton has from 8 to 9 wires per inch and a pitch of 180 per 27-inch width, or 53 to 61 tufts per square inch. By using a heavy 3- or 4-ply yarn to provide the necessary pile density, a dense, low-pile Wilton will generally give better service than a deep-pile, low-density weave of the same pile weight. A minimum order of approximately 200 to 500 square yards, depending on style, is normally required for custom designs.

Many mills, unfortunately, are discontinuing the manufacture of Wiltons in favor of tufted carpets that can be produced at high speeds and at a much lower cost.

Axminster. The Axminster weave was invented to imitate as closely as possible hand-knotted rug weaves. Each tuft of face yarn is individually placed, which means each one could be a different color. Where a Wilton may use up to six colors, the number of colors possible in Axminsters is unlimited.

The Axminster loom is highly organized, with each row of carpet represented by a sequence of spools of yarn that are lifted away af-

ter that row is inserted in the warp. The pile is created by inserting the yarn into the warp and securing it with a weft shot, then folding it into a "V" and cutting it. The next row is made up of a completely new sequence of spools (Fig. 23).

There is more yarn on the surface of the carpet than there is with any other carpet manufacturing method. Therefore Axminsters have the most surface pile for the amount of yarn used. Good quality Axminsters have a compact pile with excellent crush resistance.

A limiting feature of this weave is that the back is heavily ribbed and can only be rolled lengthwise.

Design Considerations. The most intricate patterns are made on Axminster looms. Color and design possibilities are unlimited. The only restriction is pile height: Variations in pile height are possible, however, by using specially treated reverse-twist yarns that "shrink" after steaming.

Specifications. Although most standard grades of Axminster have a pitch of 189, a maximum of 216 is also used. Grades can be identified by the number of tufts per square inch as follows:

1. Top-quality Axminster may have as many as 8 to 11 rows per inch and a pitch of 189, or 56 to 77 tufts per square inch.

2. Medium-grade Axminster may have 6 to 7 rows per inch and a pitch of 189, or 42 to 49 tufts per square inch. Quality can be improved by increasing yarn weights.

Axminsters have the advantage of the lowest cost for woven multicolored carpet, but large yardage orders are necessary to realize the full cost savings on custom orders.

Tufted Carpets

Tufting is the most important manufacturing technique in use today. At present over 90 percent of all manufactured carpets are tufted. Since the introduction of tufting machines in 1948, their use has increased rapidly because they provide high-speed production and lower costs for the manufacturer. The machines can operate at the rate of 550 rows of stitches per minute and can produce 20 times as much carpeting per hour as traditional looms (Figs. 24-28).

The tufting process is a simple one. It uses a needle instead of weaving mechanism to form the pile, and a prewoven backing provides the basic construction. A bank of needles as wide as the carpet inserts loops of yarn into the backing as it is fed through the machine. The loops are secured by a coating of latex applied to the back. Then a secondary backing is applied to add body and dimensional stability. Pile heights can be varied easily (Fig. 29).

Today's tufted carpets are considerably improved over those produced 20 years ago. But some problems remain. The stability of a tufted carpet is affected by the strength of the primary backing, the secondary backing, and the quality of the latex. The tightness of the surface yarn does not increase the stability, since

Figure 24. The tufting process begins with miles of tubing that guide yarn from storage to the tufting needles. A comput-erized release system keeps the yarn moving continuously. Courtesy Aldon Industries.

Figure 25. Each automated tufting machine can produce more than a million square yards of broadloom a year. Courtesy Aldon Industries.

Figure 26. *A photoelectric cell directs hundreds of needles to produce the carpet's surface pattern. The depth at which the needles thrust the yarn into the backing is controlled by the cell. Courtesy Aldon Industries.*

Figure 27. *After the dyeing process and before the drying oven, the carpet is rinsed to remove chemical residue and ensure uniform wetness so that it will dry evenly. In the drying ovens, temperatures are monitored to maintain uniformity of drying that ensures constant color levels throughout the roll. The carpet is now ready for backing, with either jute or foam cushion. Courtesy Aldon Industries.*

Figure 28. *Before the carpeting enters the finishing ovens, it is steamed and beaten to erect the pile for shearing. Huge rollers laminate the backing. Courtesy Aldon Industries.*

the primary backing is weakened during production if the needles are closely spaced. Thus tufted carpets are generally satisfactory except where a very dense construction is required for extremely heavy duty.

The backings must allow for enough stretch to permit a tight installation, but not continue to stretch out of shape as the result of shampooing or humidity changes. Synthetic backings must be able to withstand the effects of high heat during hot-tape-melt installation and not soften, distort, or delaminate. Tufted carpet's ability to conceal seams varies with the pattern.

The latex coating that secures the loops is all that keeps the tufts from pulling out. Once a tuft is pulled, it can continue to pull all the tufts in a line down the length of the carpet. A tuft bind of at least 13 pounds should be required for contract work, according to the ASTM-D-1335-67 Standard of the new HUD-FHA regulations.

Occasionally the tufting machine must be stopped to repair a broken thread or for a variety of other reasons. The resulting change in the tensions on the backing and on the threads between the machine's stopping and starting again can produce several rows of unequal height. This kind of imperfection sometimes goes undetected in the final inspections and is, unfortunately, not noticed until the carpet is installed.

Delamination of the secondary backing is a problem, especially in direct glue-down installations where

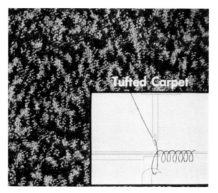

Figure 29. Tufted carpet. Courtesy Du Pont Co.

the two opposing surfaces are under different stresses. However, improved backings and laminating methods are being developed.

Design Considerations. Most tufted carpets look just like velvets, except for the slightly noticeable appearance of tufts running lengthwise. They can be level loop, cut or uncut, and can have variations of pile height that create textural patterns on the carpet surface. There are attachments for the tufting machines that can create limited textural patterns that look like random, zigzag, or embossed patterns.

Colors have been conventionally solid and moresque, similar to velvets. The printing methods of applying color and pattern can produce low-cost patterns of unlimited designs. Inventories of these patterns do not create a problem since they are printed on gray stock as they are needed.

New developments in tufting machines are producing Axminster-like

designs without printing. These innovative pattern developments reflect sophisticated technology from England and Italy as well as America.

Specifications. A high-quality tufted carpet has 7 to 10 stitches per inch in length, 8 needles per inch in width, or 56 to 80 tufts per square inch. Medium-quality tufted carpet has 5 to 7 stitches per inch in length, 4 to 6 needles per inch in width, or 20 to 42 tufts per square inch.

Custom Tufting. Custom tufted carpets are produced by a semi-manual operation that creates carpets of any size and design. They play an important role because they afford a wide range of creative flexibility.

Custom tufted carpets mean a totally original carpet can be produced to meet a certain budget and designed for a special area, unique in size, shape, coloration, pile height, and density. Custom tufted carpet can also be adapted to a design within the manufacturer's program that permits color changes, textural variations, or face weights. This is sometimes called "customized" carpet. Both custom and customized carpets are made by hand or machine depending on the intricacy of the design, the price, and the specifications.

Needlebonded Carpets
Needlebonded carpets are the modern version of ancient felted and matted fabrics. The oldest known fragment of floor covering that has been discovered up to this time is a

prehistoric scrap of felt found in a mountain cave in Turkistan and preserved in The Hermitage in Leningrad. The making of felted rugs is a major industry today in India. The method of construction still resembles the primitive one, where the dampened fibers were rolled and unrolled or pounded with stones or sticks until the fibers were compacted to form a matted layer of interlocking fibers. The same principle is used to create needlebonded carpets.

Needlebonded carpets are produced by laying carpet fibers into webs that are then passed through barbed needles that orient the fibers through the web. By repeating this process many times, the fibers become so completely entwined, compacted, and intermingled that the web is strengthened. A scrim is sandwiched in the webs to give dimensional stability and a coating of latex may be applied to the back. The weight of the fibers and the density of the felted fabric determine the wear life (Fig. 30).

Needlebonded carpets are less expensive to produce than any other textile floor covering. This is possible because there are fewer steps required to produce the final carpet. Thus less labor and time as well as manufacturing space are needed. In addition, primary backings are not necessary.

Today's needlebonded carpets are made of wool, nylon, acrylic, and polypropylene. Polypropylene accounts for over 90 percent of production. When needlebonded car-

pets are made of light stabilized polypropylene or solution-dyed acrylic, they can be used out of doors because they will not rot, mildew, or fade. They have acquired the general name of "indoor-outdoor carpet," but 85 percent of the total sales of these fibers is actually used indoors. When used outdoors, they should only cover well-drained surfaces since these carpets tend to hold water longer than others. While they do not rot or mildew themselves, a wooden floor beneath such a carpet would be subject to rot.

Originally, these needlebonded carpets were developed in 1963 by Ozite, a carpet cushion manufacturer, as low-cost weatherproof covering for miniature golf courses. Since then, they have found acceptance in a wide range of applica-

tions—from residential to all sorts of commercial use. They provide a low-cost, nonslip, floor covering that quiets, cushions, and warms concrete floors, service corridors, kitchens, and diving boards, to name a few areas not conventionally carpeted. They can be easily cut and installed and do not ravel or need binding.

The negative features have to do with appearance retention. The flat appearance and dull surface present an innocuous expanse that soon becomes very tired looking. The industry has tried to overcome this by creating printed designs, embossed patterns, and textures resembling looped pile and cut pile carpets. This helps somewhat to camouflage soiling that cannot be removed. Although they may be vacuumed easily to remove surface

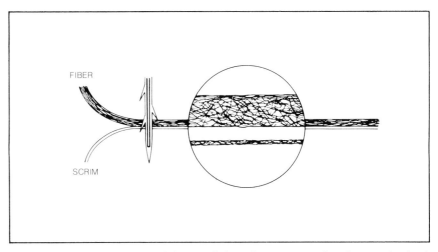

Figure 30. *A cross section of the needlebonding process showing one barbed needle. A series of needle looms with thousands of barbed needles compact the fibers into a dense fabric and bond it to a woven scrim. Courtesy Armstrong Cork Co.*

material, food and organic matter sink into the fibers and become trapped beneath the surface, leaving permanent stains.

Needlebonded carpets are appropriate and best suited for areas that have low budgets and need soft floor covering. Their application is suited to some of the following conditions:

1. Areas that need moderate sound control to help reduce clatter and a nonslip floor surface to ensure safety and reduce breakage where a quality look is not important, such as service corridors.

2. Areas where the floors are dimly lit, such as restaurants, bars, nightclubs, and theaters.

3. Areas where the installation is of a temporary nature, such as an exhibition space. The Museum of Modern Art in New York City uses needlebonded carpet in a medium gray color for its special changing-exhibit spaces where there is very heavy foot traffic. Dim light on the floors and highlighted exhibits minimize the floor's appearance. The exhibition spaces change frequently, and the carpet can be reused without much loss of yardage.

Knitted Carpets

There seems to be no general agreement about the origins of knitting. It appears to have been introduced in Europe by the Arabs by the 5th century A.D. Knitting, both by hand and by machine, has always been an im-

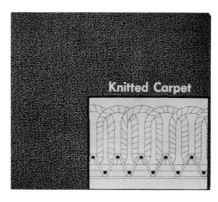

Figure 31. *Knitted carpet. Courtesy Du Pont Co.*

portant textile process in the United States.

In tricot or machine knitting, loops are formed in the warp similar to those in a crochet chain, but they are connected side by side and diagonally by accessory yarn. Knitted carpets have an advantage over tufted carpets in that they utilize the yarn on the face of the carpet more efficiently. In tufted carpets almost 20 to 30 percent of the yarn is concealed and unused in the back of the carpet, while in knitted carpet the yarn forms the entire face. Face yarns and backing are fabricated in one operation.

In machine knitting a whole row is made at one time by having one needle for each loop. The row of loops that runs across the cloth is like the filling in woven carpet. The lengthwise chain corresponds to the warp. The number of stitches or loops in each square inch determines the density of the carpet. The

stiches are run-resistant and hard to unravel (Fig. 31).

Knitted carpets do not have the dimensional stability of woven or tufted carpets; they tend to stretch. The construction is like that of a sweater. The staggered diagonal loop stitch makes it a problem to have neat cross seams. The cut fabric has a ragged appearance because the yarns sprout in all directions, and seaming is not smooth.

Design possibilities are limited. Most designs are of a loop-pile texture with pile height variations possible. The surface may be randomly sheared. They are priced between woven and tufted carpets.

Loomed Carpets (Spongebonded)

Loomed carpets made with an upholstery weave and a backing of latex foam were introduced in the mid-1950s. The backing was changed in 1959 to sponge rubber, and the carpets have since found wide acceptance. They are ideal for heavy-duty traffic areas that call for glued-down installations since they provide a resilient, dense, low construction with very good acoustical and wearing properties.

They are characterized by a low-loop, tight weave that is woven through the back. The fabric is bonded or vulcanized to a sponge-rubber backing that eliminates the need for a separate cushion. Their resilience comes from the sponge cushioning rather than surface pile that is very low and dense. They can take hard wear and are easily cleaned because of their low, dense surface. The thickness and density of the sponge rubber can be varied to meet special needs. In place of the standard $\frac{3}{16}$-inch sponge base, a $\frac{1}{8}$-inch dense sponge can be used where there will be rolling carts, such as in a supermarket.

The sponge base does not allow for stretching the carpet during installations. Spongebonded carpets are laid like sheet goods and cemented to the floor with waterproof cement. In temporary installations a release cement is advisable. Seams are butted with adhesive.

Spongebonded carpets are produced in a wide variety of fibers and qualities. They can be printed or have modified Jacquard patterns. While most spongebonded carpets have low loops, they can be made in a variety of pile heights, including a high plush with a cut pile.

All spongebonded carpets are 54 inches wide and come in rolls 100 feet long (50 square yards). Special orders require minimums of 500 to 800 square yards.

Fibers

Fibers are generally classified as being either natural or man-made. The fibers used in modern commercial carpet manufacture are wool, nylon, acrylic, polypropylene, and polyester. Table 4 lists and classifies the fibers used today.

Wool is the traditional and time-tested fiber used from the earliest history of carpet construction because the early rug makers were nomad sheep herders. Since then, rug making has been associated with the technology of the wool industry. This legacy of tradition and standards forms the basis with which all other fibers are compared.

Wool is a raw material that is in diminishing supply as the world's demand for it increases. The search for plentiful low-cost fibers that can be used in place of wool has led to the growth of the synthetic fiber industry. Synthetic fibers can be "engineered" to exhibit special qualities for specific purposes in the end product. The ideal fiber has yet to be engineered despite the claims of the chemical industry, the carpet manufacturers, and an army of public relations representatives. And the search goes on.

The inspiration that lead to the development of synthetic fibers came to an English scientist, Robert Hooker, in 1665 from his study of silk worms. Although further experimentation took nearly two centuries, the creation of artificial filaments in 1842 utilized the basic principle of spinning monofilaments that is being used today. Liquid is forced through a nozzle or spinneret with fine holes to form filaments. This liquid, or dope, is formed by the polymerization of small, simple molecules into a larger macromolecule, whose properties are different from the basic units.

Synthetic fibers are used in over 80 percent of the carpets made today because of their uniformity, durability, ability to hold vivid colors, resistance to fading, and relative price stability. More information on fibers can be found in the section on fibers in Chapter 1 that discusses filament yarns, staple yarns, yarn counts, deniers, and ply. Table 5 summarizing the assets and drawbacks of each fiber is shown at the end of this chapter on pages 58–59.

The future of synthetic fibers will be affected by more rigorous federal flammability regulations, the establishment of biological smoke tolerance standards, and the effects of shortages in the petrochemical industry. How the industry responds to the first two pressures will depend in good measure on persistent consumer demands. For a full discussion of this issue, read Chapter 6 on flammability.

Shortages in the petrochemical industry will undoubtedly result in higher prices, reflecting increased costs and limited availability of the basic raw materials used to make synthetic fibers. The basic raw materials include *benzine* as well as *ethane* and *propane*.

Benzine that becomes cyclohexane and caprolactane is the major ingredient in nylon. A chemical cousin to

TABLE 4. SOURCES OF FIBERS

Natural Fibers

Plant	Bark: redwood, mulberry
	Stem: flax, hemp, ramie
	Leaf: sisal, pineapple, abacá, palm leaves
	Fruit: coconut husks (coir fibers)
	Seed hairs: cotton, kapok, milkweed
	Sap: rubber
Animal	Sheep: wool
	Camel: vicuna, alpaca
	Goat: mohair, cashmere
	Silkworm: silk

Man-made Fibers

Mineral	Asbestos
	Fiberglass
	Gold
	Silver
	Copper
	Stainless steel
Regenerative	Cellulose: rayon, acetate, triacetate
	Protein: soybean (soylon), casein (aralac)
Synthetic aromatic	Condensation reaction: polymide (nylon), polyester
Aliphatic	Additive reaction: acrylic (vinyl, nitrile), urethane (polyurethane), olefin (polypropylene)

benzine is para-xylene, an essential ingredient with ethylene glycol in polyester. These are sometimes classified as *aromatic fibers*. Benzine is in demand as an octane-control material used to replace lead in gasolines.

Ethane and Propane that form acrylonitriles are the basis for acrylics. Propane is converted to propylene, and with ethylene it is made into polypropylene (olefin) fibers. Ethane and propane fibers are sometimes classified as *aliphatics* because they are derived from natural gas. Ethane is converted to ammonia and is in very short supply because of the worldwide need for fertilizers, and propane is in demand as a heating and cooking fuel.

Wool

The wool culture has been developing since 4000 B.C. The Babylonians had an active wool trade, and by 2500 B.C. wool growing was a major industry in Mesopotamia, whose sheperds developed knotted pile carpets famous throughout the world. The Persians and the Greeks developed sheep raising, and the Romans spread this knowledge through Europe. They introduced wool manufacturing into Britain in 55 B.C., where it prospered, and sheep to Spain where breeding developed the famous Merino stock. In fact Merino sheep were the commodity that was taxed that gave Ferdinand and Isabella the income to finance Columbus's voyages. After

that, Spanish sheep were brought to America, and under Spanish domination the Navaho Indians developed into sheperds and weavers. Spanish sheep were also introduced into South Africa and Australia where important flocks developed.

Spain and England were rivals in the production of wool as well as trade during the Middle Ages. When England finally became the world power, Britian's wool industry relied on her overseas colonies to supply raw materials and markets.

Today's domestic United States wool production is unsuited for carpet use, and all carpet wools are imported, coming from different sheep breeds, climatic conditions, and countries, such as Scotland, New Zealand, Argentina, Pakistan, and China. These wools are blended to provide the characteristics required for performance: resilience, wearability, dyeability, and soil resistance. All wool used in carpet manufacture in this country is treated with permanent moth proofing to protect it against any vermin, moth, or beatle damage.

Physical Characteristics. Wool is the fiber of a living animal, a protein product. The outer surface is a series of serated scales that help the fibers cling together. The center of the fiber is composed of spindlelike cells that supply elasticity and strength. The molecular construction of wool is in the form of a coil-like chain that resists crushing or bending. This gives wool natural

elastic recovery. Wool can be stretched from 25 to 35 percent of its original length without breaking, and it can be bent 20,000 times without breaking—making it extremely flexible.

Wool has moderate abrasion resistance similar to most acrylics. It is not as strong as nylon, polyester, or polypropylene. At least twice as much fiber weight is required for wool to wear as well as nylon. Therefore, to increase wool's abrasion resistance, it is very successfully blended with staple nylon, which results in a very hard-wearing carpet. The blends are 20 percent nylon with 80 percent wool or 30 percent nylon with 70 percent wool.

Dyeability and color fastness of wool are highly satisfactory. Color fastness is not as good as that of some solution-dyed acrylics and polypropylenes in sunlight, but it is generally better than that of nylon.

Wool is a high generator of static electricity, second only to nylon.

Wool excels the synthetics in hiding and repelling soil because of its surface structure. It is permeated with natural oils which reject dry and waterborn soil so that soil can be removed effectively. This helps it to maintain its appearance longer.

Wool is damaged by chemicals and bleaches, but most commom stains can be removed easily with mild detergents. It is unaffected by mineral acids, resistant to organic solvents, and generally resistant to weak, cold acids. It scorches at 400°F and chars at 572°F.

The natural flame resistance of wool is an asset. The damage that a lighted cigarette or match can do is limited in area, and the resulting char can easily be scraped away, leaving almost no trace. Synthetics, however, melt and fuse with heat and leave unsightly scars.

Performance. Despite its weakness in durability, wool continues to be a favored fiber. Experience with wool carpets in contract installations is consistent, dependable, and predictable. With the correct specifications for the location, wool carpet should perform with the least risk. It is resilient, resists soiling, and has good texture retention, good cleanability, good appearance retention, and excellent flame resistance. When blended with nylon, it has excellent wearability in heavy-duty situations. Soft and warm, it is unmatched in situations calling for a luxurious carpet. In qualities above $15.00 a yard, wool is unquestionably preferred, especially in custom carpets.

Mohair has recently been introduced as a luxury carpet fiber. It is an animal fiber from Angora goats, which are domesticated and originally come from Turkey. The goats thrive elsewhere only in South Africa and the southwestern United States.

Mohair is a beautiful fiber that adds opulence and luster to carpets. It appears to be the ideal fiber that combines all the qualities desired in a carpet. It is a coarser, more wirey fiber than wool and has great resiliency. It possesses great tensile strength and has a distinctive lusterous sheen. It is easily cleaned, resilient, durable, and beautiful. However, there is insufficient information about actual performance to make conclusive statements about it. Both its price, which is 3 times the price of wool, and its limited availability have hindered its application.

Nylon

A laboratory accident lead to the discovery of nylon, the most outstanding and widely used synthetic fiber today. In 1927 the E. I. du Pont de Nemours and Company started a fundamental research lab in their chemistry department. In studying polymers the chemists tried to remove molten polymers from a vessel and found that they left long fibers. After much more study, the new fiber was introduced to the public in 1938 as toothbrush bristles, in 1939 as hosiery, and in 1958 as bulked continuous filament for carpets. In the 1960s newer forms were introduced, and carpet yarn was developed with unique soil-hiding properties. A high-temperature-resistant form of nylon was developed called "Nomex." Other manufacturers have developed additional soil-hiding forms of nylon as well as antistatic forms.

Physical Properties. Nylon is the generic name for a group of polymids of two types—type 6 and type 66. They have slightly different properties, yet they perform similarly. Nylon's outstanding property is its unusual strength. It is stronger and weighs less than any other carpet fiber; therefore less fiber is necessary in construction. It resists abrasion and is very hard wearing.

It is moderately resilient. Its resilience comes partially from heat-set crimping. In low-pile constructions it will show less wear in traffic lanes than other fibers.

Nylon absorbs very little moisture, and this nonabsorbent quality makes nylon resist some dyes. Prolonged exposure to sunlight will cause some degradation and fading, which affects its appearance over a period of time. Soil-hiding continuous filament nylons retain their color longer than other forms. Some fibers are now solution dyed. The fibers decompose in strong mineral acids and are soluble in phenol and formic acids.

Nylons generate more static electricity than any other carpet fiber. Many forms of static control are possible to help solve this problem. Du Pont plys stainless steel filaments with the nylon prior to tufting or weaving and has developed an antistatic form of "Antron" (Fig. 32). Rohm and Haas manufacture a modified nylon yarn, "X-Static," that acts as a conductor, Monsanto adds a chemical modififer to their nylon, "Cadon," to reduce static build-up, and Allied Chemical has developed an antistatic form called "Anso-X." Static control treatment also includes humidity control and special chemical sprays that are applied to the installed carpet.

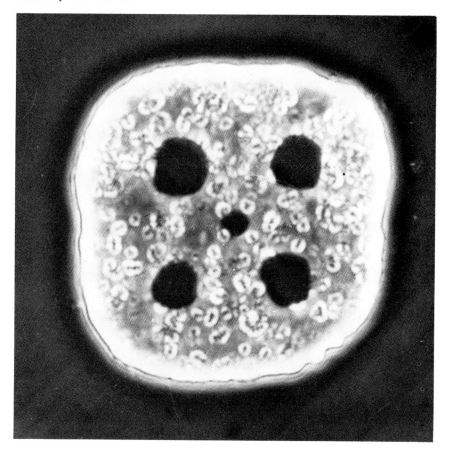

Figure 32. Microphotograph of a cross section of filament "Antron" nylon used in carpets. Courtesy Du Pont Co.

Nylon carpeting is noted for its high rate of soiling. Because of its static qualities and its optical properties, soiling became a major problem in the development of nylon fiber. The soil that was left clinging to the fibers after vacuuming was magnified by the light going through the fiber. Soil build-up was exaggerated by this process.

The new forms of soil-concealing nylon solve this problem in various ways. Du Pont pierces the fiber with interior holes that break up and dis-burse light going through the fiber so that the optical effect is altered. Allied Chemical modifies the shape of the fiber to accomplish the same thing, and Monsanto put additives in their nylon that dull the light going through.

Nylon stains less readily than wool. If stains are treated quickly, nylon carpeting has good cleanability.

Nylon is a thermoplastic fiber that will soften, melt, and fuse at high temperatures; for example, it melts at 414° to 480°F. A cigarette ash is more than 500°F and can easily melt nylon. Many constructions will pass federal flammability standards (see Chapter 6 on flammability). In fact "Nomex" has been developed to withstand very high temperatures; it will not melt but will decompose at 700°F.

Experience. Nylon is the most versatile synthetic carpet fiber. Its great durability and exceptional resistance to abrasion make it very desirable in contract situations. The soil-hiding, antistatic forms are preferred.

It performs better than other yarns in place of very hard wear such as pivot points in corridors, in front of counters, at the entrances of buildings, or where wheeled equipment is used, such as in libraries and hospitals. These are typically situations requiring low, dense pile carpet.

Continuous filament nylon fibers are ideal for heavy-duty wear as they do not pill or fuzz. Staple nylon forms pills that stay on the surface attached to loop pile textures; therefore they are used for cut pile carpets and with wool blends.

Nylon takes the widest range of colors and can be dyed by the greatest variety of technical methods.

Acrylic

The search that resulted in the discovery of nylon led to the development of other synthetic polymers. There are two forms of acrylic fibers used in carpeting: acrylic and modacrylic. In 1950 these fibers were first sold under the name of "Orlon." They are spun by the same process as nylon. The chief difference between acrylics and modacrylics is that modacrylics are fire resistant. Modacrylics are also softer and less resilient than acrylics. Therefore, modacrylics are chiefly used in blends to add their fire-retardant properties.

Physical Properties. Acrylic filaments are first spun from a solution and then spun into yarn only in staple form. Before spinning into yarn, the filaments are crimped and chopped into lengths. The crimping and spinning produce a bulky, soft quality, with good flexibility and resilience that give acrylan a wool-like hand. However, its high bulk leads to overexpectations. The yarn weight must be at least that equivalent to wool for standard performance. Acrylics can be compared with wool in bulk and also in abrasion resistance, but in actual use, wool appears to be slightly more durable. Acrylics have tensile strength, and the short ends of fiber that come to the surface and form balls are hard to wear away.

Acrylic fibers are highly resistant to sunlight and weather as well as many chemicals, which makes them ideal for indoor-outdoor carpets (Fig. 33). They take dyes very well, and in solution-dyed form they are exceptionally colorfast. The colors are clear and vibrant when dyed before extrusion. Their brightness and sparkle do not last, however, as a deposit of soiling builds up with use, and the clarity is not restored with cleaning or shampooing.

The appearance of acrylic carpets steadily diminishes with wear. They resoil quickly after cleaning and do not return to their original appearance. However, the fibers resist moisture absorption, and some stains are easily removed if they do not penetrate through the backing.

Acrylics produce the lowest level of static electricity of all the fibers.

Modacrylic fibers stick together at 275° to 300°F and acrylics stick at 420° to 490°F. They have good resistant to mineral acids and common solvents. Modacrylics are unaffected by alkalis, but are soluble in warm acetone.

Experience. Acrylics have been available since the 1950s, and they have been changed and improved since that time. The fibers have a soft, warm, luxurious hand comparable with wool, but wool is slightly more durable. Acrylic carpeting has excellent color retention and low-static levels, but it does not resist soiling and quickly resoils after shampooing. It is not as strong as nylon and has only fair texture retention.

Polypropylene

The newest of the man-made fibers is polypropylene or olefin. Polypropylene polymers form the filament that becomes the olefin fiber. In 1961 the Hercules Corporation developed a textile-grade olefin, and since then olefin fibers continue to be constantly improved. One chemical- and stain-resistant olefin fiber that was developed with low-static qualities is called "Vectra."

Physical Characteristics. Polypropylenes are exceedingly strong fibers similar to nylon, with great tensile strength, abrasion resistance, and durability. They have a low-static build-up, second only to the acrylics. They have poor resilience, and newer forms are now being crimped and heat set to allow wider styling possibilities.

Polypropylenes are impervious to stains and chemical reactions, and they do not absorb water. The fiber has excellent resistance to most acids and alkalis, and it is generally soluable above 160°F in chlorinated hydrocarbons.

Olefin fiber comes in both continuous filament and staple form that can be piece or solution dyed. Colors are dull by comparison with those of other fibers, and the color range is limited. Solution-dyed polypropylene is as colorfast and fade resistant as solution-dyed acrylic, and it can be compared with acrylic in its colorfastness and low-static build-up.

Polypropylene has a very low softening range (285° to 330°F), and as a result it can fuse and scar more easily than other carpet fibers. For example, the heat produced by friction, such as that produced by moving a heavy object over the surface, might scar the carpet. It is not con-

sidered flammable because it melts rather than burns.

Experience. In widespread use since 1962, polypropylene has become synonymous with outdoor carpeting. It is chemically inert and stainproof, and can be used successfully in laboratories. It is hard wearing, but has poor resilience, poor texture retention, and a dull appearance. Because of the problems of texture and resilience, it is well suited to needlepunch carpets and very low pile carpets. It is specified in the same face weights as nylon.

Polyester

Polyester development was part of the research Du Pont laboratories initiated in 1927 that spawned a whole family of synthetic fibers. One form was developed by Du Pont into nylon, and another form was developed by British scientists into polyesters. The first British fiber in this series was called "Terylene." It was first sold in this country as "Dacron" in 1951. The trade names for polyesters now used in carpets are "Fortrel," "Kodel," "Vicron," as well as "Dacron." These carpet fibers continue to be improved to meet the needs of heavy-duty wear.

Physical Characteristics. Polyesters are long-chained polymers of certain esters, and they are used in staple yarn form to create a spun yarn with a wool-like esthetic. Polyester fiber is highly durable—3 times more so than wool—but has poor re-

silience and crushes easily in foot traffic. It also soils easily, but is easily cleaned. The third generation of polyesters that have just been developed were designed to overcome these shortcomings. Du Pont's Dacron III has been structured to have a trilobal cross section to hide soil build-up and an increased crimp to resist crushing and provide added resilience. It is as static prone as wool and can be woven with static-control yarns.

Polyester takes color well. It can be piece or stock dyed. Its colorfastness is superior to that of nylon and equal to that of yarn-dyed acrylic and wool.

With very good resistance to mineral acids, some forms of polyesters are affected by concentrated sulfuric acid. Polyester fibers decompose in alkalis at the boiling point. They are generally insoluable in common solvents but soluable in phenolic compounds.

Experience. Polyester carpet fibers appear to be potentially appropriate for contract use, but the new forms have not been available long enough for definitive evaluation. They do promise to fill the market's need for wool-like softness and luxury but at a lower cost. Polyester fiber is lower in cost than branded acrylic fiber and less is required in the face weight to give comparable service. The fiber is more durable than wool or acrylic and still retains a soft, luxurious hand. It has good colorfastness and responds to different dye methods.

Table 5 summarizes the assets and drawbacks of the fibers discussed above.

Fiber	Assets
Wool	Best soil resistance
	Good cleanability
	Good texture retention
	Flame resistant, self-extinguishing
	More resilient than acrylic, polyester, or polypropylene
Nylon	Most durable, hard wearing
	Maintains its appearance
	Very good texture retention
	Good cleanability in soil-hiding forms
Acrylic	Excellent colorfastness
	Low static level
	Good stain resistance
Polypropylene	Very durable, hard wearing
	Excellent stain removal
	Low static level
	Fade resistant
Polyester	More durable than acrylic or wool
	Good stain removal
	Clear colors

TABLE 5. THE CHARACTERISTICS OF CARPET FIBERS AND THEIR APPLICATION

Drawbacks	Application
Most expensive fiber Not as durable as synthetics Static level high Not all stains can be removed	General use Luxury custom carpets
Static level very high Will melt and fuse with heat Poor colorfastness	Heavy traffic areas (such as hospitals, schools)
Poor soil resistance Easily resoiled Less durable than other synthetics Pilling hard to remove Will fuse with heat	Moderate traffic areas Indoor-outdoor use
Poor texture retention Poor resilience Limited colors Melts and fuses with heat	Heavy traffic areas Indoor-outdoor use (such as laboratories, utility areas, ramps, corridors)
Poor resilience Static level high Poor soil hiding Melts and fuses with heat	Moderate traffic areas

Beneath the Surface

The great undercover story of what goes on beneath the carpet surface is an unglamorous mystery. It deals with three hidden elements: backings, installations, and cushions. These three are interrelated and incestuously intertwined. Who can say where carpet backings leave off and become their own cushion? Who knows what happens in the dark between the primary and secondary backings?

Backings

The backing fabrics of the carpet, both primary and secondary, give dimensional stability to the carpet surface, prevent buckling, and add greater depth to the carpet. The added depth is an aid in seaming and supplies a cushioning effect that enriches the surface and strengthens the back, both of which add to the wear life of the carpet.

In tufted carpets the primary backing is the vehicle of construction and contains the tufts. Latex is used to secure the tufts to the primary backing and provides the adhesive for the secondary backing (Fig. 34).

Backing fabrics until about 1964 were mostly natural fibers—jute or cotton. While the use of jute as a primary backing has diminished since then, it is still the preferred secondary backing. Jute is popular because of its dimensional stability and its ability to stretch. This stretchability ensures good installations. Jute performs well when seams are either sewn or hot-melt taped. Since it is insensitive to heat, jute will not soften or distort during the process of hot-melt taping. In direct glue-down installations it absorbs and accepts the adhesive well, making for a secure bond, and it allows some adhesive to penetrate to the primary backing to ensure greater bonding.

The disadvantages of jute are that it shrinks when wet and can leave a brown or yellow stain on the carpeting face. There are also problems of adequate supply. Because jute has to be imported from Pakistan, which means that shipments can be held up by dock strikes or political conflicts and are subject to fluctuations in price, the use of synthetic backings has increased.

Added incentive for the development of synthetic backings is the fact that market projections for future needs of carpeting seem to outstrip the available supply of jute.

Synthetic backings are made of polypropylene and are both woven and nonwoven. They were specifically developed for use in the tufting and needlebonding process that require a stronger backing. These synthetic backings are waterproof and nonabsorbent, and when combined with synthetic fibers that are colorfast, they produce completely weatherproof indoor-outdoor carpets.

Woven synthetic backings provide needed stretchability, but they have the following disadvantages:

1. Closely spaced tufting stitches weaken and distort them, and they can tear with wear.

2. They are heat sensitive and not suitable for printing and dyeing procedures that require high heat and steam.

3. Their heat sensitivity creates problems in applying cushion-type secondary backings.

4. They fray and ravel in cutting and seaming.

5. Their heat sensitivity creates problems with hot-melt seaming applications.

6. They ravel under power stretching during installation.

Nonwoven synthetic backings seem to have been developed without some of the disadvantages listed above. They have a limited amount of stretch, but they do not ravel. They are dimensionally stable, and will take closely spaced stitches. They are available in two grades: one is a lighter weight to be used with a secondary backing, and the other is a heavier version especially designed as a unitary backing that eliminates the need for a secondary backing. The unitary backing is being promoted for use with both direct glue-down installations and installations over pads. It would appear to eliminate one of the major problems with tufted carpets—that of delamination of the two backing fabrics. Once a carpet has been delaminated, it is impossible to achieve dimensional stability, and the carpet

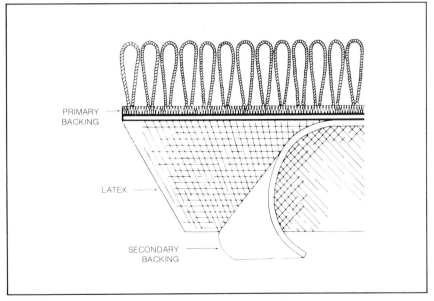

Figure 34. A cross section showing carpet backing composed of a primary backing, latex, and a secondary backing. Courtesy Bigelow Carpet Co.

CONVENTIONAL TACKLESS

buckles and distorts. A firmer cushion should be used with a unitary backing to eliminate stresses.

Installations

There are three forms of carpet installations (Fig. 35): direct glue-down carpet, carpet with attached cushion, and carpet with separate cushion (tackless installations).

Direct Glue-down. The installation of low-loop carpets applied directly to the floor without a separate cushion or an attached cushion (Figs. 36 and 37) has met with great success and interest since it was first introduced in 1965. That year the initial large-scale installation was made in the Ford Motor Company building in Dearborn, Michigan. As this type of installation has grown in popularity and success over the years, the following conclusions can be drawn:

1. It is an alternative to hard-surface floor covering, but it does not have the plush feel underfoot that is usually associated with carpeting over a cushion.

2. It is recommended for areas where there is a great deal of heavy rolling traffic, such as with library book trucks, mail carts, and food service wagons (Figs. 38 and 39).

3. It is recommended for ramps and sloped areas where carpet stability is required.

4. It is recommended for large open areas where conventional tackless installation cannot achieve optimum stability.

CARPET WITH ATTACHED RUBBER BACK

DIRECT GLUE DOWN

Figure 35. Methods of installation. Courtesy Bigelow Carpet Co.

5. Resilience and acoustic and thermal insulation are secondary to traffic demands that require this type of installation.

6. It can be installed over already-existing resilient tile and floors with only slight preparation.

7. There is easy access to under-floor duct systems, floor power outlets, and telephone equipment. United States Steel Corporation's 64-story headquarters that opened in Pittsburgh in 1969 uses strips of carpet over ducts with release-type adhesive and standard adhesive for the balance of the carpet.

8. Tighter and more durable seams are easier to obtain, but they must be sealed or they will ravel. Carpet seams are less likely to open as there is no shifting of the carpet.

9. Carpet goes down before partitions go up, which results in increased speed of office installation and easier rearrangement of office space.

10. With increased mobility for wheels and casters, the need for chair mats is eliminated.

11. Large back-shop areas can benefit from the physical and psychological contributions of capet.

12. Installers and dealers must follow the manufacturers' recommendations for procedures and materials. The installer, the dealer, and the mill all share legal responsibility for their products and services, but the problems of delamination and

Figure 36. *Glue-down installation. After one piece of carpet is pressed into the adhesive and the bubbles are rolled out toward the seam area, seam adhesive is applied to this open edge. Courtesy Du Pont Co.*

Figure 37. *After the entire seam is butted together under compression, excess ripple is worked away toward an uncemented area, leaving a joining that is virtually undetectable. Courtesy Du Pont Co.*

Figure 38. Glue-down installation in the computer center of the Ford Motor Credit Co. Heavy carts moving around the clock have not loosened the carpet or separated the seams. Courtesy Jute Carpet Backing Council, Inc.

Figure 39. Direct glue-down carpet is unaffected by heavy moving equipment and fork-lift trucks in the plant of Consolidated Controls Corp., Bethel, Conn. Carpet installation was possible here without removing the existing crumbling asphalt tile. Courtesy Jute Carpet Backing Council, Inc.

the proper adhesives should be the responsibility of the manufacturer.

13. The carpet face wears at a faster rate than when carpeting is installed over a cushion. Therefore carpet life of a glue-down installation is somewhat shorter. This can be offset by using a very hard-wearing fiber.

14. The choice of backing, whether synthetic or jute, seems to matter very little except that the jute backing usually remains intact when the carpet is removed.

15. One of the major drawbacks of this method of installation is the difficulty of removing the carpet. Release cements are being developed by various companies, whose primary purpose is to leave the floor in good condition rather than provide for reuse of the carpet, since little of it can be used again. The user should expect to leave the carpet on the floor throughout the life of the carpet.

Carpet with Attached Cushion. Contract carpets are available both with and without attached cushions. Carpets that are usually stocked with attached cushions can be ordered without the cushion.

The techniques of installing cushion-backed carpets require mechanics who know the sophisticated special handling that is required. The contract for the installation should contain protection against unsatisfactory workmanship and guarantee that all material meet flammability requirements.

One of the problems in installing cushion-backed carpets is the difficulty in seaming. Invisible seams are hard to produce. The seams have a tendency to open up with use as a result of gradual fatigue of the cushion. Seams also open up as adhesives fail to hold under the pressure of heavy traffic.

Seaming layouts must be very carefully worked out since the carpet cannot be stretched to meet installation conditions. Usually additional carpet is required to fill in the places where conventional carpet could be stretched to fit if necessary.

Most cushion-backed carpets are available in widths beginning at 54 inches. The cushions are from ⅛ to ¼ of an inch thick and are usually ³/₁₆ of an inch.

There are three types of attached cushions: sponge rubber, foam rubber (or latex foam), and vinyl foam.

Sponge Rubber is the most preferred product. It has the thickest cell walls and is heavier than foam. It is made from a solid and is chemically stable. Sponge rubber must be applied to the carpet by lamination or vulcanization. It can only be laminated in widths up to 6 feet.

Foam Rubber is made from a liquid mix and is mechanically frothed. It is spread on the back of the carpet at a controlled thickness and is then cured in an oven. It can be applied to broadloomed carpets of 12 and 15 feet. The resulting carpet costs less than sponge-backed carpets.

One problem with foam is that it is a mechanically created substance

that has a tendency to decompose as the frothy material returns to its original state through wear. The quality of foams also varies widely. Another problem is that the heat required in the curing may alter the surface texture of the carpet, particularly with acrylics, and there may be some scorching of lighter colors. Thickness of the finished backing is not always consistent.

Vinyl Foams have been available for a while. They are the lightest backing in weight and do not decompose. But they are by nature a hard material that must be made to adhere to a soft carpet backing. The addition of plasticizers to the vinyl unfortunately results in hardening and cracking of the backing.

Carpet with Separate Cushion (Tackless Installation). The installation of carpet over a separate cushion is the best-known form of installation and the most trouble free. It provides the following advantages:

1. It increases the sound-absorbing acoustical properties of carpeting (Figs. 40 and 41).

2. It provides thermal control of heat and cold.

3. It extends the life of the carpet pile and helps retain its texture.

4. It improves comfort underfoot.

Installation follows established methods. Tackless stripping is installed at the outer edges of the room or area to be carpeted and is filled in with the cushion; then the

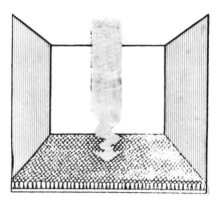

FLOOR SOUND ABSORBTION

carpet is kicked or power stretched into place.

There are many qualities and constructions of carpet cushions available. They should be chosen on the basis of the type of traffic expected. For commercial and institutional installations, a soft surface is undesirable and a firm or extra-firm cushion that is flame retardant should be selected. A more luxurious feeling from a soft cushion would be appropriate in some private offices, lounges, and board rooms. In grade school classrooms where children sit, read, or play on the floor, a soft cushion would make the carpet more enjoyable.

Cushions

There are three types of cushions or pads available.

1. Natural hair and fiber blends are described according to weight in ounces per square yard. They are permanently moth proofed and sterile, and they are suitable for all above-grade installations. The all-hair 40-ounce cushion is outstanding as an all-purpose cushion with excellent wear life, and it does not support combustion. Additional cushioning and resiliency can be provided with additional weight, a waffle surface, or the addition of a layer of rubber. Hair and fiber cushions tend to mat down with time and can become mildewed.

2. Foam and sponge-rubber cushions were discussed in the preceding section on carpets with at-

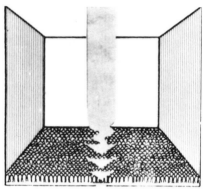

IMPACT SOUND TRANSMISSION

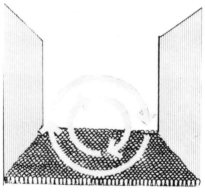

SURFACE NOISE REDUCTION

Figure 40. Sound conditioning. Carpet absorbs about 10 times more sound than other types of floor covering. Courtesy Bigelow Carpet Co.

tached cushions. They are available in flat sheets and perform the same as when they are attached to the carpet. They are more expensive than hair and jute pads, but they retain their resiliency longer. They usually come with the top surface bonded to a burlap fabric to facilitate

even stretching of the carpet. Not all rubber cushions meet flammability requirements.

3. Homogeneous urethane cushions with extremely fine cell structure are a recent development. These remarkable new materials were discovered through foam technology. They are high-density, homogeneous polymeric foam, with excellent durability and strength. They are laminated to a nonslip surface that gives dimensional stability and resistance to abrasion, and they are available in residential and contract densities. Their advantages are that (a) they have superior sound-insulating properties; (b) they do not shred or ravel; (c) they are unaffected by moisture or heat and will not oxidize, crumble, or deteriorate; (d) they will not elongate or delaminate; (e) and they meet both the Hill-Burton Act and the Department of Commerce flammability standards (see Chapter 6 on flammability). Olin's "Omalon" and General Felt Industries' "Breakthru" are examples of this type of cushion.

There is another cushion product that does not fit into any of the above categories: Du Pont's "Pneumacel" is a compressed mat of polyester fibers. The polyester material is made of millions of microscopic closed cells that are permanently inflated with inert gas. This pneumatic structure provides excellent cushioning and long-term durability. It also meets flammability requirements.

Figure 41. Impact noise rating.* Courtesy Du Pont Co.

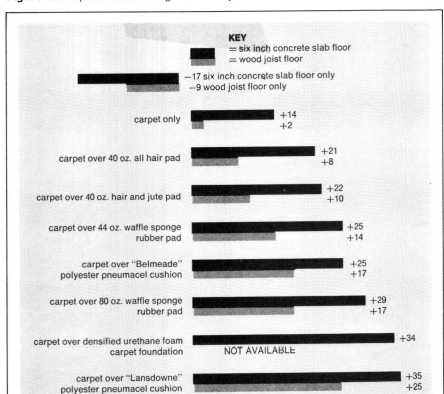

KEY

■ = six inch concrete slab floor
▨ = wood joist floor

−17 six inch concrete slab floor only
−9 wood joist floor only

carpet only +14
+2

carpet over 40 oz. all hair pad +21
+8

carpet over 40 oz. hair and jute pad +22
+10

carpet over 44 oz. waffle sponge
rubber pad +25
+14

carpet over "Belmeade"
polyester pneumacel cushion +25
+17

carpet over 80 oz. waffle sponge
rubber pad +29
+17

carpet over densified urethane foam
carpet foundation   NOT AVAILABLE +34

carpet over "Lansdowne"
polyester pneumacel cushion +35
+25

*Tests conducted by Kodaras Laboratories, Elmhurst, New York, in accordance with FHA 750; carpet used was 40-oz pile woven wool carpet. Numbers are in decibels; 2 decibels is the significant difference level.

PART II

ASPECTS OF
PERFORMANCE

Static
Control

Static control is no longer the luxury it used to be before the rapidly increased use of air conditioning. Today's commercial buildings, more and more often constructed with sealed windows and year-round air conditioning, help create climatic conditions that increase static. Static results from the rapid discharge, to a ground, of voltage built up on a body—for our purposes an example of this is what happens when a person walks on a carpet. Because most people object to any shock received from walking on a carpet, the most compelling reason to control static discharge is for human comfort.

But with the increasing use of carpeting in industrial buildings and institutions, static electric discharge must also be controlled because it affects the functioning of some sensitive electronic equipment. Some computers have been upset by an extremely fast transient current, some heart monitors have malfunctioned because of a static charge, and there has been danger from a spark in the presence of oxygen tanks. Since the phenomenon of static build-up and discharge can be described and measured, several methods are being developed to deal with it. Carpet manufacturers are making safety adaptations by introducing humectants or fine conductive wires into the fibers during the manufacturing process. Anti-static sprays are being produced. Institutions are using equipment with interference filters that is not so sensitive to static discharge. Hospitals are using nose tubes that do not present the same problems as oxygen tents.

Static Build-up

Static build-up is the result of repeated rubbing and separation of shoes on carpet pile, and it is caused by the difference in physical properties of the two materials. The friction of rubbing two different materials together generates a charge that is felt as a shock when a person touches another object. The *magnitude* of the charge is the result of charging and discharging. Charging is related to:

1. The effective conductance and dissipation in the horizontal plane of the carpet.

2. The conductance of the carpet through the backing and underlay to the building ground.

3. The conductance of the shoe surface from the person to the carpet pile.

4. The conduction of ions in the air. A person walking across a carpet builds up static voltage with each step. When humidity in a room is low, there is not enough moisture on the face fibers to conduct electrical charges. Higher moisture levels result in greater ion mobility and therefore faster discharge; the charge is dispersed into the carpet instead of building up in the person.

The number of variables that can af-

fect the magnitude of the charge include:

1. The environmental conditions, like temperature and relative humidity. Extremely dry conditions promote static build-up (Fig. 42).

2. Differences between people, such as weight, posture, and manner of walking. The voltage generated can vary from person to person and with the time of day.

3. Generic fiber types. The surface shape of the fiber, or its moisture-absorbing characteristics, affects its static propensity. Every fiber is capable of producing static and is affected by the processing chemicals and dyes. The hard surface of nylon and its low absorption make it the highest static producer.

4. Carpet construction, yarn spinning, backing materials, underlay, and even the base flooring material.

5. Wear, soiling, and cleaning.

6. Shoe sole material. There is a wide range of voltage generated with various types of shoe soles. The Brunswick Corporation conducted the standard Carpet and Rug Institute (CRI) Shuffle Test on several different fibers in contract carpet constructions using different sole materials. The results are shown in Table 6. They indicate the wide range of static build-up, from 1,000 to 13,000 static volts, for oak-tanned leather, neolite, and chrome-tanned leather soles. Statistics from the Tanners Council show that oak-tan-

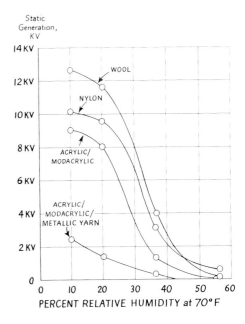

Figure 42. *Effect of humidity on static generation of level-loop contract carpets (CRI stroll tests with leather sole shoes). Courtesy Dow Badische Co.*

TABLE 6. STATIC PROPERTIES OF FIBERS *

Static volts	Shoe Sole Material		
	Oak-tanned leather	Neolite	Chrome-tanned leather
13,000	Nylon Wool		
12,000		Nylon	
11,000		Wool	
10,000			Nylon
9,000			
	Acrylic		
8,000			Polypropylene Acrylic
7,000	Polyester		Wool Polyester
6,000			
	Polypropylene		
5,000			
4,000		Polyester Polypropylene	
3,500 3,000 2,500		THRESHOLD OF SENSITIVITY	
2,000			
1,000		Acrylic	

*All carpet fibers produce static. Table shows static properties of various fibers without added static control. The term "threshold of sensitivity" refers to the range of voltage where people actually begin to feel static. The tests were made at 20 percent relative humidity, 70°F.
Courtesy The Brunswick Corp.

ned shoes are 17.7 percent of all shoes manufactured in the United States, neolite composition soles are 82 percent, and chrome-tanned leather shoes are 0.3 percent.

Methods of Control

Static control is possible when the charge built up by the individual can be dispersed into the carpet at a reasonable rate. There are two general mechanisms that can be used to draw the charge away from the person: *ionic conduction* and *metallic conduction* (Fig. 43).

Ionic Conduction acts with the presence of humidity. There is greater ionic mobility when there is additional moisture and therefore a faster discharge.

Environmental humidity control is a desirable way to ensure ionic conductivity. The introduction of moisture in the air at high, but comfortable levels reduces static generation to the comfort level.

A humidifier is a possible, but not always an economical, solution. Antistatic sprays are also available. They act to absorb and retain moisture in the carpet's surface pile and reduce static by ionic conductivity. Temporary in nature and easily reapplied on site, antistatic sprays have proven to be effective, but with limitations. Often they diminish in usefulness with abrasion and shampooing, and some attract soiling. They should only be applied to clean surfaces.

Figure 43. Static control reduces static electricity build-up below the threshold of human sensitivity, 2,500–3,000 volts. There are three ways to control static: left, increase relative humidity; middle, introduce static-reducing materials and conductive backing during manufacturing; and right, apply antistatic spray. Note: *there is no static-free carpet; test results are not precise; test conditions are not always reproducible.*

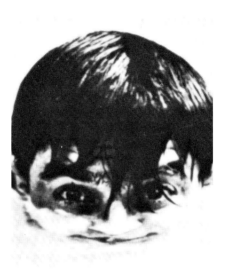

INCREASE RELATIVE HUMIDITY

COPPER WIRE

CONDUCTIVE YARNS

APPLY ANTISTATIC SPRAY

ZEFRAN (with Zefstat)

BRUNSLON

LOW-STATIC YARNS

CONDUCTIVE BACKING

Figure 44. *Brunslon plied into three-ply yarn. Courtesy Du Pont Co.*

A recent development by fiber producers is the incorporation of a humectant into the fiber. Chemicals are added to the molten nylon or polyester fiber that control body voltage at medium- to high-humidity conditions. With the addition of a conductive backing, the humectant is also effective at lower humidity levels. At present no polymeric product functions well at humidity levels below 30 percent relative humidity.

Metallic Conduction is the most effective form of static control available today. The introduction of a fine conductive wire into the pile yarn of the carpet (Fig. 44) effectively maintains a low level of static, no matter what the shoe soles material. The wires need not be grounded. They work by dissipating the charge over the entire surface of the carpet. The wires must be woven into the surface pile and come in contact with the shoes.

Metallic conductors are used in such forms as slit metalized film, fine wires, metallic core fibers, or short-length metal filaments. All apparently succeed in holding static below the perceptible limits and retain their effectiveness for the life of the carpet.

The Dow Badische Company has

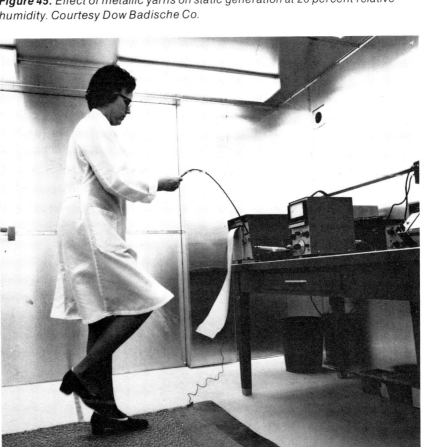

investigated the effects of different sole materials on acrylic blend and nylon carpets, both with and without metallic threads. The introduction of metallic threads effectively lowers static charges in all cases (Fig. 45).

Copper, aluminum, and stainless steel threads are used for metallic conduction. Copper wires have esthetic drawbacks as they are visible in the pile, and they have a short wear life due to copper's softness. Aluminum is used as the core metal of a monofilament yarn made by Dow Badische that is inconspicuous and strong. The most successful antistatic metallic wire is stainless steel. It is a very fine filament, one-sixth the diameter of human hair. It is effective and easily camouflaged.

Wear, soiling, and cleaning affect the permanence and performance of all static-control measures.

The specifier need not recommend a particular system of static control. But needs only stipulate that the antistatic element last the life of the carpet and that the static build-up not exceed 2,500 volts at 20 percent relative humidity at 70°F, which is the threshold of human sensitivity as tested by AATCC 134-1969. To ensure the best performance, a value below 2,500 static volts should be specified (Fig. 46).

Figure 45. *Effect of metallic yarns on static generation at 20 percent relative humidity. Courtesy Dow Badische Co.*

Figure 46. *Static test. Carpet sample is tested in an aluminum-sheathed environmental room at Allied Chemical's Technical Center. Courtesy Allied Chemical Corp.*

Flammability

Still a hot issue, current flammability regulations and testing methods are the subject of much confusion. It is only recently that flammability has become a subject of debate in Congress, in the carpet industry, and among fire safety officials. Until recently most carpets were made of wool, which is self-extinguishing. The confusion comes partly from the increasing use of carpeting in buildings subject to fire safety standards and partly because synthetic carpets have been involved in fires in which lives were lost.

The controversy revolves around the question of what test to measure flammability with and which government agency to listen to. The Department of Health, Education, and Welfare (HEW) recognizes the Steiner Tunnel Test, and the Department of Commerce recognizes the Methenamine Pill Test. Both tests have been criticized on their validity to measure hazards in real situations. A changing patchwork of state and local regulations adds to the general confusion.

Essential to the flammability issue is the central concept that the carpet be fire retardant. Low-loop, dense construction generally passes strict flamespread tests. But when the carpet surface gets higher, lighter, and more plush or shaggy, the chances of meeting the flamespread tests lessen. The carpet industry knows its customers want all kinds of carpets, and they cannot produce them and meet the requirements of the Flammable Fabrics Act of 1969 and the Hill-Burton Act of 1965.

The Flammable Fabrics Act applies to all carpeting. It sets up the Federal Flammability Test that all carpets and rugs must pass before they can be sold to the public. Not only do manufacturers have problems meeting these standards, but the Federal Trade Commission has trouble enforcing them.

Carpets meeting the Hill-Burton requirements are readily available. Reputable carpet manufacturers test their carpets and publish the ratings. Those carpets that pass are usually low-loop constructions. Problems arise when specifiers want to use other forms of carpeting.

Chronologically the situation developed as follows.

1965

The Department of Health, Education, and Welfare began a review of the tests available to measure potential fire hazards of carpet materials. They adapted a test originally devised by Underwriters Laboratory because it was the only test for flamespread on interior finish materials that was nationally recognized. HEW applied it to carpeting in hospitals and nursing homes receiving funds under the Hill-Burton Act. It is commonly referred to as the Steiner Tunnel Test (Figs. 47 and 48).

The tunnel test ratings of carpet assemblies (carpet underlays and adhesives) for Hill-Burton set standards of a flamespread index of not more than 25 points for exits and 75

points for other areas, as tested according to ASTM-E-84.

The tunnel test was originally devised for testing building materials like floor tile or wallboard. Carpeting is tested in an upside-down position by exposure to a jet of flame at the top of a tunnel. Because it is not tested in its original position and because themoplastic fibers melt and drop to the floor of the furnace exposing more carpet to the flame, many people are dissatisfied with the test.

1969

The Department of Commerce issued a flammability standard for carpets under the provisions of the Revised Flammable Fibers Act. The Federal Trade Commission's Bureau of Consumer Protection is charged with enforcing the Flammable Fibers Act. The Department of Commerce issued Document DOC-FF-1-70 as the standard for the surface flammability of rugs and carpets and Document DOC-FF-2-70 as the standard for small rugs and carpets. These standards were developed by the carpet industry in cooperation with the National Bureau of Standards.

The test method has become known as the *pill test*, or Methenamine Tablet Test (Figs. 49 and 50). It consists of a methenamine tablet placed in the center of a piece of carpet 9 inches square, over which is placed a piece of steel with an 8-inch diameter hole. The pill is ig-

nited. If the charred area does not extend to within an inch of the edge of the hole, the carpeting meets the acceptance criteria. Critics of this test say that the pill provides a very small ignition area and it does not produce enough heat to engage the backing.

The essential differences between the two tests are

1. The pill test measures the reaction to a small ignition source, such as that from a match.

2. The tunnel test measures the reaction to a front of flame, such as that produced by a building fire.

The General Services Administration adapted the pill test standard for all government purchases under Document DDD-C-95.

Toxic Smoke a New Problem. One month after the Department of Commerce issued its flammability standards, there was a tragic fire in a Marietta, Ohio nursing home that attracted national attention. Thirty-three of the forty-six Medicare patients died. The fire broke out in a plastic wastebasket, presumably from a discarded cigarette. Dense smoke developed, and the elderly patients were led or carried out.

The fire spread rapidly and generated suffocating smoke. Officials said that it was the carpet that contributed to the spread of the fire. The carpet had a nylon face and was bonded to black foam rubber. It was apparent that the nylon carpet melted in the room where the fire

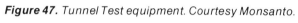

Figure 47. Tunnel Test equipment. Courtesy Monsanto.

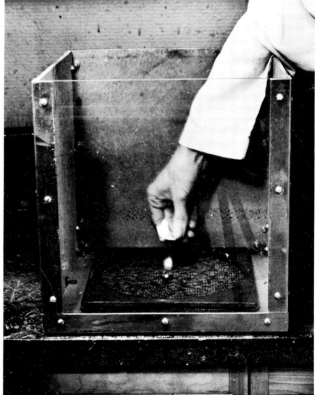

Figure 49. *Equipment used to determine carpet flammability by means of the Methenamine Tablet Test. Courtesy Monsanto.*

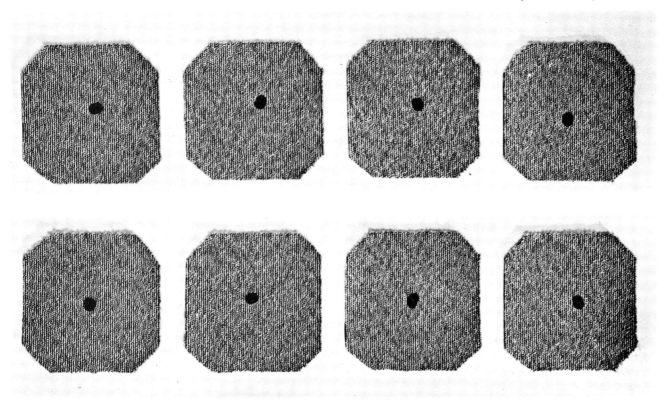

Figure 50. Eight Tablet Test specimens of an identical carpet after testing. If a specimen burns 3 inches in any direction, it fails the test. For a carpet or rug to be acceptable under the standard, not more than one specimen of the eight may fail. Courtesy Monsanto.

started. The deaths were not caused by the spread of the fire, but by the smoke and noxious gases generated by the burning rubber padding under the carpet.

The carpet had a flamespread rate of 275 in the tunnel test, almost 4 times the Hill-Burton maximum of 75 for patient rooms and more than 10 times the 25 rating for exits. However, the same carpet met the criteria of the pill test, and would have been acceptable to the Department of Commerce.

The problems of ensuring life safety can be lessened considerably by systems designed to detect smoke and heat and by sprinkler systems that turn on automatically after room temperature reaches a regulation high level. Although attention focused on the carpeting in the aftermath of the Marietta fire, as yet there has been no legislation requiring the installation of detection or sprinkler systems in nursing homes, hospitals, or office buildings.

1970

The Social Security Administration has authority over nursing homes and Medicare facilities, and prior to this year, it has not had a flammability standard. The administration received a lot of criticism in Congress as a result of the Marietta fire, and consequently, it adopted the tunnel test for new facilities, but it has not taken a stand on existing facilities.

1971

The Federal Register published regulations regarding fire and safety standards called the Life Safety Code. It is a consensus standard for protecting people from the hazards of fire. It adopts the tunnel test as the method of testing carpets in accordance with the National Fire Protection Association Standard No. 225 and ASTM 84.

1972

The Department of Commerce promised to develop new standards to surpass the pill test, but they were not announced this year. In the revised federal specification for carpeting DDD-C-0095-A (GSA-FSS) of March 1972, the pill test was still specified. Current fire safety regulations standards for furnishings and appliances are listed in Table 7 and for building and construction in Table 8.

1973

HEW is still looking into the development of smoke-generation test standards.

Smoke Standards Needed

Up until now little attention has been paid to a most serious aspect of the flammability question: the lethal effect of the smoke of synthetic fibers. Since this smoke can be as deadly as any poison gas planned for war-

fare, there is a need for biological smoke-tolerance standards to safeguard against toxic exposure.

An important study, the first of its kind to draw attention to the effects of burning synthetic fibers, was presented in 1973 to the American College of Surgeons by Dr. Donald P. Dressler of the Harvard School of Medicine and reported in the *World Medical News* of Nov. 9, 1973. Dr. Dressler and a research team that compiled the very sobering report were working under a grant from the National Institutes of Health in the field of heart and lung research. They investigated the possibility that the combustion products of synthetic fibers might be partially responsible for the death of some 5,000 people who die annually of smoke inhalation.

They exposed 750 rats to smoke produced by wool, acrylic, and nylon rugs as well as by white pine. The smoke was comparable in quantity with that made by burning 1 square yard of material in an average bedroom.

"The rapidity with which unconsciousness and death occur—often in less than two minutes—is startling and frightening," warned Dr. Dressler. He noted that lethal smoke from acrylic and nylon carpeting rendered the animals unconscious so fast that if people breathed comparable amounts it "could preclude their escape." Wool and wood smoke had delayed effects and did not always prove fatal.

Table 7. Fire Safety Regulations Standards for Furnishings and Appliances *

Issuing agency/ regulation	Coverage	Typical limits	Sources of further information
Department of Commerce	Carpets larger than 24 sq. ft.	Flame spread less than 3 inches in any direction. (DOC FF 1-70).	Office of Flammable Fabrics, Federal Trade Commission, 11th St. & Pennsylvania Ave., Washington, D.C. 20234. Also Ofc. of Flammable Fabrics, National Bureau of Standards, Washington, D.C. 20234
	Small rugs and carpets.	Same as above (DOC FF 2-70).	
	Mattresses.	Char length less than 2 inches from cigarette ignition source (DOC FF 4-7).	
Department of HEW, Hill Burton Office	Floor finish, carpeting in federally funded hospitals.	Flame spread rating of 75 max. (ASTM E 84, UL 273).	General Standards of Construction and Equipment for Hospitals & Medical Facilities, Public Health Service Pub. No. 930-A-7, Superintendent of Documents, U.S. Govt. Printing Office
Department of HEW, Social Security Adm.	Floor finish for nursing homes.	Flame spread of 25 max. to 200 max. (ASTM 84, UL 723).	Federal Register, Vol. 36, P. 20675, Oct. 28, 1971
Port Authority of New York and New Jersey	Carpet assemblies.	Flame spread of 25 max. to 150 max. (ASTM E 84).	Port Authority of New York and New Jersey, 111 Eighth Ave., New York, N.Y. 10011
	Upholstery materials and plastic furniture.	Upholstery self-extinguishing in vertical burn (Fed. Spec. CCC-T-191b, Method 5903).	
		Padding flame spread of 100 max. (ASTM E 84 & ASTM E 162).	
	Plastics (self-supporting.)	Self-extinguishing in vertical burn (Fed. Spec. CCC-T-191b, Method 5903).	
Local Building Codes	Interior hangings, curtains in public assembly areas.	Self-extinguishing in vertical burn test, char limits. (ASTM D-626, NFPA Std. No. 701, Cal. Health & Safety Code Title 19).	Local building codes; Title 19, State of Cal., Documents Section, P.O. Box 20191, Sacramento, Cal. 95820
City of Boston	Solid plastic chairs, desks, shelves and upholstery coverings. padding and cushioning.	Self-extinguishing under conditions specified (BFD tests 11-1, 11-2, 11-3, 11-4, ASTM D 635).	Boston Fire Dept., Fire Prevention Headquarters, 115 South Hampton St., Boston, Mass.

Test methods

Designation	Property measured	Information source
DOC FF 1-70 **DOC FF 2-70**	In carpets, measures flame spread from burning hexamethylene tetramine tablet.	Ofc. of Flammable Fabrics, Federal Trade Commission, 11th St. & Pennsylvania Ave., Washington, D.C. 20234
DOC FF 4-72	In mattresses, measures ability of mattress to resist ignition by burning cigarette.	Also Ofc. of Flam. Fabrics, National Bureau of Standards, Washington, D.C. 20234
ASTM E 84	Flame spread by 25 ft. tunnel (same as UL 723, NFPA 255, UBC 4201 and ANSI A2.5—1970)	ASTM, 1916 Race St., Philadelphia, PA 19103
ASTM E 162	Flame spread determined at 60° under radiation conditions.	
ASTM D 635	Horizontal burning rate of rigid plastics over 0.050" thickness.	
Fed. Spec. CCC-T-191b, Method 5903	Measures flame propagation, afterglow and char of fabrics in vertical burn.	General Services Adm., Specifications Activity, Printed Materials Supply Div., Bldg. 197, Naval Weapon Plant, Washington, D.C.
California Health and Safety Code Title 19 (para. 1237.1, 1237.2 and 1237.3)	Measures afterflame and afterglow or char in vertical burn tests.	Local Building Codes Title 19, State of Ca., Documents Section, P.O. Box 20191, Sacramento, CA 95820
Boston Fire Dept. Tests 11-1, 11-2, 11-3, 11-4	Measures ability of product to self-extinguish under conditions of test.	Boston Fire Department

Note: The information shown here is subject to change. Please check for current regulations with the issuing agency.

TABLE 8. FIRE SAFETY REGULATIONS STANDARDS FOR BUILDING AND CONSTRUCTION *

Issuing agency	Coverage	Typical limits	Sources of information
Local Bldg. Codes	Walls & ceilings in high-rise, institutions, general assembly occupancies	Fire-resistance index of 1-2 hrs. (ASTM E 119, UL 263)	Local building, plumbing, electrical codes; also BOCA Code, Uniform Bldg. Code, Southern Std. Bldg. Code, and National Building Code
	Interior finishes, thicker than 1/28" over non-combustible substrates	Flame spread of 25 max. to 200 max. (ASTM E 84, UL 723)	
	Interior hangings, curtains in public assembly buildings	Self-extinguishing in vertical burn test. Char length as specified (ASTM D 626, NFPA 701)	
	Plastics	Flame spread of 225 max. (ASTM E 84, UL 723). Smoke of 75 max. (UBC Std. 52-2)	Uniform Building Code
		Burning rate limits (ASTM D 635, ASTM D 568)	Southern Building Code
NFPA Std. 101; Life Safety Code *	Fire-resistive walls in exit hallways and stairwells	Fire-resistance index of 0.5 to 2 hrs. (ASTM E 119, UL 263)	National Fire Protection Assoc., 60 Batterymarch St., Boston, Mass. 02110
	Interior finish	Flame spread of 25 max. to 200 max. (ASTM E 84, UL 723)	
Dept. of HUD, Federal Housing Administration	Walls, columns, beams, floors, stairways, all construction	Fire resistance rating of 3/4 to 3 hrs., depending on occupancy. (ASTM E 119, UL 263)	HUD Minimum Property Standards, Superintendent of Documents, U.S. Government Printing Office, Washington, D.C. 20402
	Interior finish	Flame spread of 25 max. to 200 max. (ASTM E 84, UL 723)	
Dept. of HEW, Hill-Burton Office & Social Security Administration	Walls, columns, beams, stairways of hospitals and nursing homes	Fire resistance rating of 1-2 hrs. (ASTM E 119, UL 263)	General Standards of Construction and Equipment, for Hospital & Medical Facilities, Public Health Service, Publ. No 930-A-7, Superintendent of Documents; and Federal Register, Vol. 36, p. 20675, Oct. 28, 1971
	Interior finish of walls, ceilings	Flame spread of 25 max. to 200 max. (ASTM E 84, UL 723)	
	Floor finish materials	Flame spread of 25 max. to 200 max. (ASTM E 84, UL 723) **	
Dept. of Commerce	All carpeting larger than 24 sq. ft.	Flame propagation less than 3" (DOC FF 1-70)	Office of Flammable Fabrics, Nat'l. Bu. of Stds., Wash., D.C. 20234 or Office of Flam. Fabrics, Fed. Trade Comm., 11th St. & Pa. Ave., Washington, D.C.
Dept. of Labor, OSHA	Same as NFPA Std. 101	Same as NFPA Std. 101	National Fire Protection Assoc., 60 Batterymarch St., Boston, Mass. 02110

Test Methods

Designation	Property measured, general description	Source
ASTM E 84	Flame-spread rating determined on ceiling of 25 ft. tunnel (same as UL 723, NFPA 255, UBC 42-1 and ANSI A2.5-1970)	American Society for Testing & Materials, 1916 Race Street, Philadelphia, Pa. 19103; Underwriters' Laboratories, Inc. Publications Dept., 207 E. Ohio Street, Chicago, Ill. 60611
ASTM E 119	Time for burn through of a wall, floor or other structure (same as UL 263, NFPA 251, UBC 41-3, and ANSI A2.1-1971)	
ASTM D 568	Self-extinguishing and burning rate properties of vertical plastic sheets and film less than 0.050" thick, Bunsen burner ignition	
ASTM D 626	Maximum char length after exposure of bottom edge of vertical strip to a burner for 12 sec. (similar to NFPA 701)	
ASTM D 635	Horizontal burning rate of rigid plastic over 0.050" thick, Bunsen burner ignition.	
DOC FF 1-70	In carpets, measures flame-spread distance from standard burning hexamethylene tetramine tablet.	Office of Flammable Fabrics, National Bureau of Standards, Washington, D.C. 20234 or Office of Flammable Fabrics, Fed. Trade Comm., 11th St. and Pennsylvania Ave., Washington, D.C. 20580

*Even though standards such as model building codes and Life Safety Codes are not regulations per se, they are often incorporated with little or no modification into codes by local, state and federal authorities.

**Hill-Burton flame spread 75 max. compulsory; SSA limit of 25 to 200 max. not compulsory, but enforceable at discretion of authority of jurisdiction.

Note: The information shown here is subject to change. Please check current regulations with the issuing agency.

The importance of the report is summed up in Dr. Dressler's words: "These studies of the biological effects of smoke on animals clearly demonstrate that the indiscriminate use of plastic building and decorating materials may result in hazards to people." Dr. Dressler stressed that biological smoke-tolerance standards for synthetic carpeting must be established. "Tests for flammability alone, obviously are no longer adequate to safeguard our families."

We can hope for two developments in the future: One is that the fiber producers will introduce relatively nontoxic fibers, and the other is that federal standards will be broadened to include biological smoke tolerances.

Tests and Performance Standards

Test methods can be used to evaluate carpeting. In fact they are the only way to objectively measure the carpeting characteristics we are discussing here. These tests for carpet performance are designed not only to enable carpet mills to develop and produce carpets that will conform to a given quality, but also to help a specifier evaluate a carpet by comparing it with known standards. A specifier can request that a carpet meet certain standards by spelling out those standards in terms of performance test levels (Figs. 51 and 52).

Test methods do not measure actual conditions, but they do try to approximate them through simulated laboratory situations. For instance, time can be accelerated, and individual qualities can be studied. These tests have been developed by the technical experts in the industry, and they are used to measure levels of performance. Table 9 lists the most frequently used test methods.

Testing procedures used to judge conventional carpet have been standardized and accepted by government, industry, architects, and designers. Test standards established by the carpet mills, fiber producers, and The Carpet & Rug Institute are the lowest minimum acceptable standards so as to allow the greatest number of products to be covered. They do not necessarily insure the best performance in actual use. The level of performance that is expected must be determined by the specifier.

The Federal Supply Service of the General Services Administration publishes a set of specifications and performance test standards used by all federal agencies:

1. Carpet and Rugs, DDD-C-95 (0095A), Mar. 15, 1972.

2. Carpet and Rug Cushions, DDD-C-00123, Dec. 22, 1966.

3. Carpets and Rugs with Attached Cushion, DDD-C-001559.

4. Textile Test Methods, CCC-T-191.

The Department of Housing and Urban Affairs (HUD) has developed a carpet certification program for FHA use: HUD's Use of Materials, Bulletin UM 44c (Carpet Standards). HUD sets standards for conventional carpeting, woven or tufted shags, and carpets used in housing for the elderly and emphasizes in the standards the types of traffic the carpets will be exposed to.

Further information about testing methods and standards can be obtained from the following sources:

American Society for Testing Materials (ASTM)
1916 Race Street
Philadelphia, Pa. 19103

American Association of Textile Chemists and Colorists (AATCC)
P.O. Box 12215
Research Triangle Park, N.C. 27709

General Services Administration (GSA)
Federal Supply Service (FSS)
Printed Materials Division
Naval Weapons Plant
Washington, D.C. 20406

Department of Housing and Urban Development (HUD)
Office of Technical and Credit Standards
Architectural and Engineering Department
Washington, D.C. 20410

Federal Trade Commission (FTC)
Office of Flammable Fabrics
11th St. and Pennsylvania Avenue
Washington, D.C. 20234

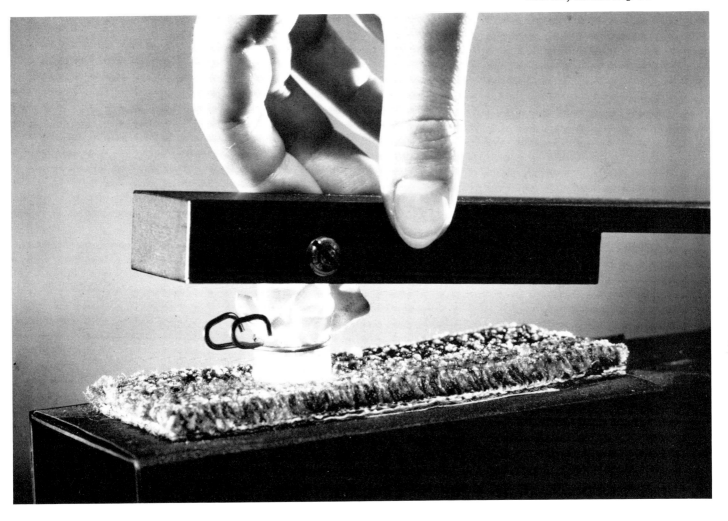

TABLE 9. TEST METHODS

Performance	Test	Description
APPEARANCE		
Service Change	ASTM D-2401	Method requires 6 mo to complete. Examination and evaluation of changes due to matting and crushing. Test simulates twisting action. Evaluation is on the extent of recovery to its prior appearance.
Shrinkage	ASTM D-138 DDD-C-95	Dimensional stability determined by simulating the effects of aging, wet method cleaning, etc. Federal spec permits 3% shrinkage for broadloom and 1% for carpet tile. Graded pass or fail.
Abrasion	ASTM D-1175	Tabor test for resistance to abrasion. Relates to durability. Must not show appreciable sign of pilling or fuzzing. Rate 4 or better based on a range of 1 to 5.
Moth and Larvae Resistance	ASTM D-116-65T	All carpets must be treated to resist larvae. Rated pass or fail.
Mildew Resistant	CCC-T 1916	Method 5762 same as for moths and larvae.
SOIL		
Accelerated Soiling	AATCC 123-1970	Used to compare the soiling propensity of two or more carpets.
Service Soiling	AATCC 122-1970	Exposure to normal foot traffic in controlled areas.
Visual Rating	AATCC 121-1970	Used to measure the accumulation of soil or the removal of soil by a cleaning method, determined by the difference in the gray scale of 1 to 5.
ACOUSTIC PROPERTIES		
Impact Noise Rating (INR)	FHA Bulletin 750	The higher the level of decibels absorbed, the better the material absorbs and reduces impact noise. The decibel level is given as the rating.
Airborne Sound Noise Reduction Coefficient (NRC)	ASTM C-423	Sound absorption coefficient indicates the fraction impinging noise absorbed by the material. Rating of 1.00 means total absorption. Concrete slab rates 0; carpet over pad rates .55.
MATERIALS		
Woven and Tufted Floor Coverings	ASTM D-418-68	Measures pile yarn weight and pile thickness.
Analysis of Textile Tear Strength	AATCC 20A-1971 ASTM D-2261-64T	Quantitative analysis of tear resistance. Minimum acceptable standard in both length and width measured according to pounds of pull: foam backed, 25 lb; glued down, 25 lb; power stretched, 25 lb.
Tuft Bind	ASTM D-1335-67	Measures how well the individual tufts are held in the structure of the tufted carpet (Fig. 45). DuPont's minimum is 15 lb.
Secondary Backing Delamination Strength	Federal Test Method 191-5100	

Performance	Test	Description
FLAMMABILITY		
Flame Spread	DOC FF 1-70	Measures flame spread from burning hexamethylene tetramine tablet (Pill Test).
Flame Spread	ASTM E-84	Measures flame spread in 25-ft tunnel (Tunnel Test).
Self-Extinguishing	Boston Fire Department: 11-1, 11-2, 11-3, 11-4	Measures ability of product to self-extinguish under condition of test.
STATIC		
Electrostatic Propensity	AATCC 134-1969	Simulates conditions under which carpet static may be produced and measured.
COLORFASTNESS		
To Light	AATCC 16-E-1971	Carpet exposed to xenon arc lamp in a fadeometer. Number of standard fading hours (SFH) changes are measured on the gray scale of 1 to 5. FHA minimum standards require a rating of 4 (good) for light colors after 40 SFH and for dark colors after 80 SFH.
Crocking	AATCC 8-1969	Measures the tendency of the dye to rub off carpet under both wet and dry conditions (Fig. 46). FHA minimum standards require a rating of 4 based on a range of 1 to 5. However, 4 indicates that some crocking, spots, smudges, and color transfer can occur.
To Water	AATCC 107-1968	Test for staining, bleeding, and color retention. FHA minimum standard is 3.5 based on a range of 1 to 5.
Ozone in the Atmosphere	AATCC 129-1971	Test for fading due to atmospheric contamination. FHA minimum standard is 4 based on a range of 1 to 5.
Ozone in High Humidity Areas	AATCC 129-1968	Developed to simulate conditions in the coast area of Florida. Standard as for ozone in the atmosphere.
Shampooing	AATCC 137-1972	Designed to simulate in-plant shampooing. Standard as for crocking. Can be used to evaluate other properties, such as dimensional changes, shrinkage, or permanency of finishes.
Rug Back Staining	AATCC 137-1972	Used to determine whether color may be transferred from the back of a colored rug to a hard surface floor.

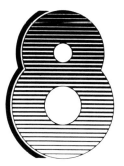

Maintenance

There are three elements to consider when selecting carpeting for institutional or corporate use:

1. Suitable carpet construction for the area

2. Proper installation

3. Adequate maintenance

Since the first two elements are discussed in Part I, let's see here what adequate maintenance involves since it is one of the most important aspects of performance of contract carpeting.

Adequate maintenance can be defined as preserving an even, overall appearance of the carpet by not allowing soil to build up in the carpet. Carpet that is heavily soiled wears prematurely. Not only is soil destructive to the carpet fiber, it affects its appearance. The carpet will look worn even though it isn't. The problem of carpet that must be replaced because of soiling is as important to the designer and the client as carpet that must be replaced because of wear. The client relies on the advice of the designer in both instances for quality and performance.

Soil Concealment

Soil concealment and camouflage are two important adjuncts to maintaining the appearance of the carpet. Color selections, used in combinations to create tweeds, texture, patterns, prints, or other soil-hiding designs, are the first aspect of the designer's approach to an area of heavy traffic. In these areas the natural earth tones of browns, reds, and grays are the most soil-concealing colors. Soil-concealing opaque fibers were specifically developed to minimize the optical exaggerations of soil build-up in nylon and polyester fibers.

Control of Tracked-in Soil

Maintenance begins with the control of tracked-in soil at the entrance of a building. Walkoff mats, grids to scrape the soil from shoes, cocoa mats, and elevator carpets are the first defenses against tracked-in soil.

Maintenance is made more difficult if there are adjacent soft and hard floor coverings to care for, and it necessitates having many types of equipment to complete the work. Carpets adjacent to the waxed floors are the most abused of all carpets. Traffic lanes in the carpet become very pronounced as the wax builds up on the fibers. The wax itself collects more dirt and grime, and the carpet mats down. Walkoff mats can help control the wax being carried onto the carpet, but usually they are not part of the designer's thinking or planning, and look like an afterthought.

Concrete stairwells and janitors' closets are other sources of soiling that can be controlled. The concrete in stairwells should be sealed before the carpet is installed and kept well maintained. Janitors' closets should have walkoff mats to control the tracking of spilled water and dusty concrete.

Maintenance Program

The purpose of a maintenance program is twofold: to retain the appearance of the carpet and to prevent soil build-up that is so destructive to its appearance and wear life. That program can be accomplished by following the steps outlined below as the situation requires.

Routine Care involves daily vacuuming or less-frequent vacuuming of areas that receive less wear. Vacuuming with a motor-driven brush and beater-type cleaner removes surface dirt from the pile and helps keep the pile refreshed. Routine care also includes additional care with extra walkoff mats on wet days, with extra walkoff mats to keep heavy amounts of soiling from reaching the carpet.

Mechanical Pile Lifters should be used once a week in heavily trafficked areas to open the pile and allow vacuuming to remove buried dirt. Not only does crushed pile trap soil and hinder its removal, but matted and crushed pile reduces the overall appearance of the carpet.

Spot Cleaning should be done as needed. Nothing is as effective for removing spots as prompt treatment. The longer a spill or stain remains untouched, the harder it is to remove. One problem is that staining agents may react with the carpet dyes and result in permanent discoloration. Solution-dyed fibers have the best resistance to such discoloration.

The fiber manufacturers have made recommendations for the care of their products. For instance, in their studies of various detergents, Monsanto found that there is an astounding range of effectiveness among detergents—cleaning power can vary from 0 to 54 percent of efficiency—and many well-known brands have a low rating.

An emergency spot-removal kit could contain the following items:

1. A neutral detergent solution

2. Paint remover with no oil in it

3. Dry cleaning solution

4. Rust remover

5. Acetone

6. Alcohol

7. A mild 3 percent ammonia solution

8. Acetic acid or vinegar

9. Chewing gum remover

The American Carpet and Rug Institute recommends a simple two-bottle kit for general use that contains: (1) a neutral detergent solution made with 1 teaspoon of detergent to 1 quart of water plus 1 teaspoon of white vinegar, and (2) a dry cleaning solution.

Periodic Deep Cleaning is called for when soil has built up over a long period of time. The soiling rate depends on the amount of traffic, the amount of oily grime that settles on the carpet, and the quality of the day-to-day maintenance. In general, if vacuuming and pile brushing do not restore the color and texture, the carpet should be shampooed. There are four basic shampooing methods: dry powder, dry foam, wet rotary brush, steam. The first method does not require skilled personnel for its application.

Dry Powder and Dry Foam Cleaning both have the advantage of quick drying times so that the area can return to active service within 1 to 3 hours. They can be used frequently to refresh and brighten the surface without distorting the pile. However, both are limited in their ability to cleanse heavily soiled carpet because they do not use hot water and do not penetrate very deeply into the pile. If not totally removed from the fibers, the dry powder and foam can cause rapid resoiling.

For deeper, more-thorough cleaning, the last two methods—wet rotary brush and steam cleaning—are used. They require skilled personnel and longer drying times.

Wet Rotary Brush Cleaning consists of applying detergent with a rotary brush. Then the dirty detergent should be picked up by a wet vacuum so that the suspended dirt cannot be redeposited. This is a generally satisfactory and low-cost technique that can be used on continuous filament nylons and polypropylenes, as it will not disturb their surface textures. However, pile distortion can be a problem with other fibers. Additional problems are that underscrubbing may lead to streaks and uneven cleaning; and overwetting can cause shrinkage of the backing, seam splitting, and browning, as the color of the jute bleeds through to the surface.

Steam Cleaning is generally regarded as the most effective and efficient method of thorough on-site carpet cleaning. A preheated detergent is applied under pressure and injected into the pile, and the machine immediately extracts the soiled solution. Steam cleaning does not distort the pile while it effectively removes soil. There is no residue of detergent to collect dirt.

Both rotary brush and steam cleaning can potentially shrink any carpet backing that is subject to shrinkage when saturated. But if the carpet is fastened properly around the perimeter, there should be no shrinkage problems. If moisture penetrates the seams and they are properly made, they should hold. Failures do sometimes occur with improperly made hot-melt seams, but this is an installation problem, and the carpet can be repaired.

Table 10 summarizes the on-site and in-plant methods of carpet cleaning that have been discussed.

Importance of Detergents

Without detergents not ony would the job of removing a single stain but the cleaning of the carpet of an entire building would be much harder. Detergents emulsify soil and oil particles and suspend them until rinsed away. However detergents that remain behind in the cleaning process cause more rapid resoiling to occur. They may remain in the fabric if they were not rinsed away fully enough, or they may dry to a waxy or oily residue and cling to the fibers. Any foam or powder detergent that ends up as a powder can be an effective surface brightener only if it can be completely vacuumed away.

A simple test will demonstrate what is left on carpet fibers after using foams, powders, or liquid detergents. Put small amounts of those detergent solutions in flat dishes and allow them to evaporate. Check the residue with your finger. If it feels sticky, waxy, or oily, it will attract soil. The best detergents for carpet cleaning dry to a crisp dry powder that can be vacummed away easily.

Wet Detergent Shampooing removes deeper soiling. The hotter the water, the greater the detergent's cleaning ability, regardless of the fiber. Heat increases the molecular activity and produces a physical agitation between the detergent solution and the soil particles that dislodges the soil. The water temperature should be 140° to 150°F. Neutral detergents with a pH of 7 to 8 are recommended for safe use with wool and for spot removal from all fibers. More alkaline detergents with a pH of 8 to 11 are recommended for synthetic fibers. The higher the alkalinity, the greater the chance of leaching stains from the jute backing.

TABLE 10. METHODS OF CARPET CLEANING

On-site Cleaning Method	Evaluation of Method	Drawing of Method
STEAM EXTRACTION Based on injection of a jet of hot water containing detergents at a prescribed rate and then extraction by a vacuum system.	Does excellent cleaning. No pile distortion or flaring. Built-in vacuum removes soil. No residue of shampoo to collect more dirt. Excellent pile restoration.	
CYLINDRICAL BRUSH– DRY FOAM In one pass a cylindrical brush scrubs and picks up the foam generated by the machine.	Causes severe pile distortion and flaring of tufts. Has a built-in vacuum that removes shampoo and dirt.	
ROTARY BRUSH– WET SHAMPOO A rotary brush uses wet shampoo. A complete set of accessories includes vacuum and drying equipment.	Causes severe pile distortion and flaring of tufts. Does uniform cleaning. Does not remove shampoo and soil.	
SMALL ROTARY BRUSHES– WET SHAMPOO A rotary brush cleaner that has two brushes instead of one and is somewhat smaller than the one above.	Causes severe pile distortion and flaring. Does very little cleaning. Does not remove shampoo or soil.	
SONIC CLEANING A vibrating plate gives a sonic cleaning action, causing activation of the foam.	No pile distortion. Does less cleaning than the above methods. Has no method for the removal of shampoo and dirt.	
CYLINDRICAL BRUSH– DRY COMPOUND A cylindrical brush that cleans with two rotating brushes, designed for home use.	Causes excessive pile distortion and flaring. Does less cleaning than the above methods.	

In-plant Cleaning Methods	Evaluation of Methods	
BRUSH–WET SHAMPOO and SPRAY JET	Cause some pile distortion and flaring. Do uniform cleaning.	

Courtesy The Carpet and Rug Institute.

PART III

**EVALUATION OF
SPECIFIC
INSTALLATIONS**

Hospitals

Hospitals have traditionally favored hard-surface floor coverings primarily for ease of cleaning and disinfecting. The introduction of carpeted floors in hospitals seems quite radical until one examines all the evidence that has been accumulating about the application of carpeting. Besides use in lobbies, waiting rooms, business offices, chapels, auditoriums, and conference rooms, carpeting is being used in corridors, patient rooms, nurses stations, nurseries, and dining areas (Fig. 53). It is not successful in toilets, baths, and food preparation areas.

We shall examine the application and performance of carpeting in the key areas of corridors and patient rooms, lobbies and dining areas. For this study, I visited ten hospitals convenient to me, all in New Jersey, that had carpet installations. These 10 hospitals are typical of all busy hospitals, all of which either are in the midst of a building expansion program or have just completed new facilities. They have had carpet installations of various types for differing periods of time, and there have been a variety of experiences and reactions. For example, we can take two extremes. Hackensack Hospital, after a trial period, decided not to continue carpet in patient areas, but to confine it to offices and lobbies. Contrast that experience with that of Morristown Memorial Hospital. After a trial period there, the staff recommended enthusiastically that carpet be used throughout the hospital.

The hospitals surveyed are listed

Figure 53. Carpet in hospitals is constantly exposed to all sorts of wheeled equipment. Shown here is Sunrise Medical Center in Las Vegas, Nevada, where over 8,000 yards of carpet were installed. The uncarpeted patient room is in sharp contrast: the floor appears hard and slippery and the light is glaring.
Courtesy Du Pont Co.

TABLE 11. SURVEY OF HOSPITALS *

Hospital	Location	Number of Beds	Carpeted Area
East Orange General	East Orange	285	Patient Rooms Nursing School
The Valley Hospital	Ridgewood	267	Patient Rooms Corridors
Hackensack	Hackensack	502	Offices Lobbies Dining Room
Jersey Shore Medical Center	Neptune	452	Patient Rooms Corridors Lobbies Lounges
Newark Beth Israel	Newark	519	Patient Rooms Corridors Cafeteria
Morristown Memorial	Morristown	432	Patient Rooms Corridors
Overlook	Summit	438	Patient Rooms Corridors Dining Room Lobbies
St. Mary's	Orange	228	Patient Rooms Corridors Lobbies Nursery Offices
Clara Maass	Belleville	420	Patient Rooms Corridors Dining Rooms Lounges
St. Michael's Medical Center	Newark	410	Patient Rooms Corridors

*The hospitals in this survey conducted by the author are all located in New Jersey and are listed in the order visited.

Carpet Fiber	Specifier
Wool	Purchasing
Wool	Agent
Acrylic	Architect
Acrylic	
Acrylic	Administration
Wool	
Wool	
Acrylic	Architect
Acrylic	
Acrylic	
Acrylic	
Acrylic	Architect
Acrylic	
Acrylic	
Nylon	Administration
Nylon	
Acrylic	Administration
Acrylic	
Wool	
Wool, Nylon	
Nylon	Architect
Nylon	
Nylon	
Nylon	
Nylon	
Nylon	Administration
Nylon	
Nylon	
Nylon	
Acrylic	Architect
Acrylic	

with additional information in Table II. They are all in New Jersey and are arranged in the order visited.

Performance Factors

Factors of performance discussed below are appearance, noise control, safety, microbiology, maintenance, flammability, static control, and mobility of wheeled equipment.

Appearance of a carpeted floor is consistently stated as a positive factor in the decision to put carpet in hospitals. Its natural, luxurious qualities help overcome the institutional look and help put patients more at ease. The qualities of softness and warmth produced become psychological assets. These subjective reactions as a result of the physical environment further the therapeutic goal. Mental institutions have noted the positive responses of the patient, those who care for him, and his visitors as all being influenced by the carpeted floors.

Another aspect of the appearance of carpeted floors is the reduction of glare from light on highly reflective waxed floors.

Noise Control, or the acoustical effect of sound-absorbing carpet, is another factor hospital administrators cite as being a prime asset. Resilient flooring and terrazzo, traditionally used in hospitals, have highly reflective surfaces which create reverberant spaces that tend to intensify noise. Administrators who have renovated areas with carpet are always radically impressed with the substantially quieter environment. For instance when corridors are carpeted, the clatter of carts is greatly reduced. Subdued noise gives a greater feeling of privacy despite the heavy traffic in corridors. Patients rest easier. The need for hospitals to provide relatively quiet environment is almost as obvious as the need for cleanliness.

Safety has increased with carpeting as carpeted floors minimize falls and injuries for both patients and staff.

Microbiology of Carpeting has been examined by many professional groups. The American Public Health Association and the Communicable Disease Center of the U.S. Public Health Service have conducted studies that have cleared the way for approval of carpeting. Each hospital surveyed here has also made its own studies.

Morristown Memorial Hospital seems to present a classic example of hospital concern and critical self-study. The hospital had a negative policy about carpet until they started planning a new wing for the hospital. They researched all the available material including The American Public Health Association's studies that stated that "carpet has no adverse effect on the environment as measured by microbiologic means." Those conclusions were based on tests that measured surface samples, depth studies of the carpet, and air samples, and compared the results with samples taken in uncar-

peted areas. The Infections Committee of the hospital decided to make their own study on a test floor in the hospital and made the following report in October 1971.

Based on these studies, the committee unanimously agreed to rescind the previous motion made to withhold recommendations on carpeting. Dr. Burt made the following motion: that since the bacterial count of the floors and air in rooms with carpeting are demonstrably less than those with tile, the committee recommended that carpeting be installed throughout the hospital when practicable. The motion was unanimously carried.

Similar studies have been made in many other hospitals. The Ohio State University College of Medicine's "Study of Carpeting in Nurseries" reported that

There were no demonstrable significant differences in air colony counts between the two nurseries. Colonization and infection rates among the newborn randomly assigned to the two nurseries showed no significant differences.

Based on these reported studies and others, carpet makes a very important contribution in a well-maintained hospital towards control of bacteria.

Maintenance of carpet in hospitals compares favorably with maintenance of resilient tile and terrazzo.

But in the success or failure of carpet in hospitals maintenance itself is the biggest single factor. While most hospital administrators spoke enthusiastically about the time required to vacuum carpeted areas, as compared with the time needed to maintain a waxed resilient tile floor of the same area, the problem of carpeting seems to come down to maintenance procedures. The burden in carpet maintenance must be shared between the weaknesses of the fiber and construction of the carpet itself and the willingness of a busy hospital to release the area long enough for proper shampooing and drying time. Two hospitals visited—the Valley Hospital in Ridgewood and Newark Beth Israel—had the insurmountable task of trying to maintain poor-quality carpet and poor-fiber choices. At Hackensack Hospital the entire carpet program was canceled on the basis of inadequate fiber performance.

The system of maintenance of resilient tile floors has been well established over the years. Personnel know procedures and materials and how to apply them. Because carpet is so new in hospitals, housekeepers are learning how to deal with it as problems arise. Now a new vocabulary of techniques has to be learned and used with carpeting.

It is necessary to orient and train personnel in the carpet cleaning methods. Daily vacuuming has been accepted as a standard maintenance procedure. Administrators and housekeepers report that vacuuming is easily within the abilities of their employees and that it takes less time than daily mopping and drying procedures. It is also less of a problem to maintain because both men and women vacuum easily, but women cannot manage the heavy waxing and stripping machines. However, there was no agreement about the assets or liabilities of a central vacuum system.

Spots and Stain Removal are the crucial point in maintenance. It is here that carpet fiber choice and construction are important. The newest forms of nylon, the soil-concealing ones, are very satisfactory in actual use, unlike the earlier forms of nylon. *The acrylics were the least responsive to spot cleaning and stain removal.* Wool was very satisfactory. With all fibers, the best construction is a very tight, dense, level, *low* loop to keep the soil from penetrating into the weave. Its dimensional stability should prevent it from stretching, buckling, or delaminating.

Spot cleaning succeeds with prompt attention, and most of it can be done very simply. All the hospitals try to get to a spot within 1 to 2 hours. At St. Mary's Hospital in Orange (where the entire hospital has been carpeted for the past 7 years), spots have been very successfully removed with prompt attention using vinegar, cold water, and "Joy." Spots that soak through the carpet back and penetrate the pad cannot be removed successfully and often produce odors that persist.

Carpet Shampooing is a problem. There is no agreement among the hospitals about frequency of shampooing or even of the need to shampoo. Overlook Hospital in Summit reports it does well with spot cleaning and vacuuming. St. Mary's sponges its cemented-down nylon carpet the way it would a resilient tile floor. The carpet is vulcanized to a sponge-rubber backing that has shrunk and the seams have split, but the carpet appears very clean. The problem of splitting seams may be overcome now with improved installation techniques.

Jersey Shore Medical Center in Neptune reports that foam shampoos on acrylic carpets are very unsatisfactory. They prefer steam cleaning every 6 months. In their experience, foam shampoos appear to attract rapid resoiling.

Carpet Flammability Standards at this time meet the Hill-Burton standards of the Steiner Tunnel Test that apply specifically to hospitals and nursing homes. We have discussed the regulations in Chapter 6 on flammability. For hospitals considering carpeting, there are many commercial qualities to choose from that meet federal regulations with acceptable ratings of 75, and many that rate well below this.

Static Control is important not only for computer rooms, but all sensitive patient areas. Hospitals express concern where there is oxygen mixed with other gases; where sensitive instruments were used, such as heart catheters and pacemakers; or where there may be electrical leakage from equipment in intensive care units. By grounding all equipment and using metalic threads and low-static fibers in carpeting, the problems of static electricity have been controlled. None of the hospitals has problems in this area. For instance, Clara Maass in Belleville relies on humidity control, while St. Mary's uses an antistatic spray twice a year.

Wheeled Equipment necessitates large-diameter wheels when carpeting is used. Because of this, every hospital had to make changes in their casters. Morristown Memorial Hospital decided to solve the problem of moving heavy food carts by switching to a power-driven cart, which is battery operated, safe, and quiet. The hospital is very satisfied with this arrangement, even though the cost of the motorized cart is twice that of a conventional one.

Areas Carpeted

Carpeted areas such as patient rooms, corridors, entrance lobbies, and a dining area will be discussed here.

Patient Rooms receive light to moderate traffic. The carpet need not be the same weight as that in the corridors. The problem to be met here is not wear, but spot and stain removal. Five of the ten hospitals visited had acrylic carpet in both patient rooms and corridors. Four of those were specified by the architects. *The acrylic carpets all showed stains and spots*, and the housekeepers lamented about the difficulties of spot removal and the persistence of stains long after treatment. Typical of these installations was St. Michael's Medical Center in Newark. Acrylic carpet had been down 14 months. It was an acrylic/modacrylic blend with Brunslon, in a good velvet construction, with a face weight of 42 ounces. But, regrettably, it looked quite soiled.

The exception in its choice of carpet for patient rooms was East Orange General Hospital. It was the only one to install wool. The carpet had maintained its appearance and gave a very luxurious effect to the area. The installation was a three-ply tufted wool with 48-ounce face weight and metallic thread for static control.

Corridors receive very heavy wear and should get a carpet designed for heavy traffic. A low-pile height should be maintained so that it will resist crushing, faciliate the use of wheeled equipment, and resist soiling.

Carpet in the five hospitals mentioned above that used acrylic carpets in their corridors all showed worn traffic lanes, pile crush, worn areas at corners and elevator doors, and stains. The degree of wear depended on the traffic and the age of the installation.

The newer nylons fare better in corridors. Morristown Memorial

Hospital used, in both corridors and patient rooms, a velvet construction woven through the back of 97 percent Antron nylon and 3 percent copper wire, with a face weight of 30.7 ounces and 0.250 pile weight alternating with 0.145 pile height. It was cemented down. The carpet has given excellent wear under heavy traffic conditions. The hospital feels, though, that a single pile height would be preferable because of the wheeled equipment. One problem is that the carpet has shrunk at the entrance to shower rooms where water was not controlled. Extra attention during installation could solve that problem, perhaps, with a saddle at the door to control the water.

Entrance Lobbies not only receive the heaviest traffic of all the areas of a hospital, they receive the heaviest deposit of soil and grit from the outside. A carpet in the main lobby must be able to withstand tremendous wear and the grinding effect of grit on the fibers.

The Antron carpet, described above, was installed in the lobbies of two hospitals. At Overlook Hospital it was placed where older carpet had worn through. It had been down for 5 years and showed no signs of wear except dullness of color. The carpet was also installed in the Clara Maass Hospital lobby 5 years ago and now shows signs of dullness and wear in front of the Information Desk where it is subject to the stress of pivoting abrasion. That one area is being replaced.

Dining Areas in Clara Maass Hospital's Continuing Care Unit is carpeted with an excellent soil-concealing nylon Axminster. This is an area where all the patients come for meal service. The pattern is expecially well chosen in a multicolor design that gives a cheerful, lively,·noninstitutional look to the area. The carpet should wear very successfully for many years more than the 8 to 10 years hospitals estimate for carpet wear life. This was the only hospital to select a nylon Axminster. Although the construction will give excellent wear and the pattern is very soil concealing, the problem with static control limits its application. As stated earlier, Clara Maass Hospital is using humidity control as its solution to the static problem.

Conclusions and Recommendations

1. Carpet succeeds as a floor covering in hospitals. It performs better than hard-surface floor covering except in the areas of food preparation and toilets.

2. Carpet should be cemented down where wheeled equipment is used.

3. The newer forms of soil-concealing nylon perform well in almost every situation, especially in corridors and entrance lobbies.

4. Wool can be used to great advantage in patient rooms and dining facilities.

5. Acrylic fibers are not performing

well in patient rooms and corridors.

6. The construction in all cases should be a low, dense, level loop, with static control.

7. Color selections are wide, but gold carpets should be avoided as they show soil and stains more rapidly.

8. patient rooms and corridors need not have the same weight carpet.

Schools and Universities

From kindergarden to college, from open classroom to open dormitory, educational policies about learning formats and behavior patterns have radically affected not only how students learn but the interior environments in which they study. Carpeting is one of the elements that has contributed to the changing of modern school interiors. In grade schools children use the floor as part of the learning space. Carpet transforms the floor into an active element in the learning environment. They read and work on the carpet in school the way they would at home, playing on the floor from infancy on, so that it continues to be a natural area for them.

Studies on Carpeting and Learning

The Bureau of Educational Research and Service of the College of Education at Ohio State University published the results of a study on carpeting and learning. The study was made to determine how carpeting affected the total school environment and whether or not it had any affect on pupil behavior and learning. The basic premise was that carpeting in a classroom could be justified only if it produced desirable differences in the physical environment and in the resulting behavior and learning of the pupils. It was conducted with 360 grade school pupils, teachers, and parents, and it was designed to measure achievement, personal and social characteristics, sonic environment, pupil behavior, and attitudes of pupils, teachers, and parents. The study encompassed a full school year. The summary of their report states: "The Ohio State University study revealed that carpeted classrooms provided a measurably superior sonic environment to noncarpeted classrooms and that this superiority was reflected in significantly greater student achievement only in the primary grades."

The Los Angeles City School District's study of soft floor covering made by Donald D. Cunliff in 1967 quotes this report and analyzes its own survey of teacher and parent attitudes on carpeting and custodial costs. Their conclusions are as follows:

The first reaction of most people to any statement regarding installation of carpeting in school classrooms is one of surprise coupled with a feeling that its cost is excessive as compared to that of more common floor coverings used in schools. When we use comparative costs we must determine and define the exact costs we are using.

The first or "material installed" cost of carpet floor covering is considerably more than that of resilient floor covering. However, when the floor covering is considered as only one part of a classroom of similar sonic environment, as is the present practice in the Los Angeles District, the differential is substantially reduced.

Furthermore, if average annual costs including custodial service on the basis of present District standards are to be used there is no significant difference in cost of the two types of floor covering when installed in new buildings in a manner to provide similar sonic environment of the classroom and the selection of floor covering should be made on some other basis than cost alone.

The following conclusions based on data developed in the study are among the items that should be given consideration in selection of floor coverings:

1. From the standpoint of the teachers, the sonic environment in the classroom with carpeted floors and painted hard-surface ceiling is superior to classroom with resilient floor covering and acoustic tile ceilings.

2. Carpeting the second floor of two-story wood frame buildings solves the problem of noise transfer to first-floor rooms and no sound insulation blanket between floors is necessary when carpeting is used.

3. The general appearance level of carpeted floors in our schools is much higher than for vinyl asbestos tile. This is largely due to the problem of rubber burn marks on the resilient tile flooring.

4. At first there is some hesitancy on the part of teachers and students in performing regular class-room tasks, such as using tempera colors, etc., but this is quickly overcome after the carpet has been in use a short time.

5. Teacher reaction indicates that they believe the carpeted room is more conducive to learning.

Design and Performance Considerations

Many schools and colleges have become disenchanted with carpeting after an initial trial period. They have complained that the carpet has not lasted and its appearance and performance have been poor. The following four points are possible reasons for disappointing results with carpeting:

1 Dissatisfaction can be traced back to improper selection and/or poor maintenance.

2. When budget cuts are made, they are usually reflected in cheaper carpeting and cutbacks in maintenance equipment and personnel.

3. Price is frequently a factor in carpet selection rather than performance characteristics.

4. Often decisions are made by people who are handicapped by not having sufficient technical information to make carpet selections appropriate for the areas.

Primary considerations when choosing carpeting should be:

1. Resistance to Wear and Crushing. School traffic is concentrated in narrow traffic lanes that develop in corridors and corners and around fixed workareas. Loose carpet construction and fibers that don't resist crushing will result in a worn matted carpet.

2. Ease of Maintenance. Soil build-up quickly reduces the appearance life of a carpet. Control of tracked-in soil with extensive use of walkoff mats and grids to catch soil from muddy shoes coming in from playing fields is a necessity. Color choice and a concealing pattern will work to conceal soil. Fiber choice and construction must provide an easily cleaned surface.

3. Installation. There are a variety of situations in schools that call for different installations. Direct glue-down installations work well in libraries where heavy bookcarts must be pushed easily, in corridors and classrooms where the desks and chairs are shifted, and on ramped aisles of auditoriums and lecture halls. Carpet over pad should be used where children and teachers sit on the floor to play or read. The added cushioning and thermal qualities add to the pleasure of the carpet. Carpet over pad should also be used where sound suppression is important, such as in music practice rooms, lounges, dormitories, offices, and corridors.

Installation in areas not previously carpeted includes places such as gymnasium walls. Carpet there acts to absorb sound as well as impact. Playgrounds might also be improved with carpeting. An indoor-outdoor carpet in areas where children run and jump would make a safer play area.

Carpeted Areas

The areas that are carpeted in schools and colleges vary from small applications in individual rooms to completely carpeted buildings. Room-size areas of carpet are found in classrooms, libraries, and offices.

Isolated spots of carpet like area rugs are used in kindergardens and home economics rooms. These could be patterned or textured high-pile carpets that will withstand moderate traffic. A soft, colorful carpet that promotes a homelike feeling is ideal in these locations.

Schools. Two New Jersey schools are discussed here.

The Village School in Holmdel carpeted its open plan area and library in 1971. Mr. Paul Evans, the principal, supported by enlightened, involved, and interested parents, made a study of carpets before they made their decision. Various carpets were tested for wear, resiliency, and color. Several manufacturers submitted samples that they considered appropriate for school use. There was a wide range of fibers, piles, and textures. The school's carpet committee finally decided on a solution-dyed continuous filament nylon, in three colors—avocado, Spanish olive, and Indian curry. The avocado showed the least soiling. The carpet was glued down because the committee felt it would facilitate moving furniture easily in the open plan areas. The teachers now feel that the carpet should be softer and warmer for the children to sit on. In spite of that the school is very satisfied with the carpet. It finds the maintenance very easy and economical with just daily vacuuming.

The Broad Street School in Matawam installed an olefin carpet at the architect's suggestion, throughout the corridors and open classrooms of a renovated school. This carpet was installed over a pad and is a comfortable and warm surface. The gold color is good and shows no sign of fading.

There was some crushing from the furniture in the open classrooms, and in several areas the tufts along a row of stitches have pulled. There is a curious buildup of chalk dust at the blackboards that cannot be removed with vacuuming or shampooing. Spot cleaning is difficult, lipstick is the worst stain, and unfortunately it was carried through the school on the soles of shoes. The all-over appearance, however, is good after 3 years, even at areas of extreme wear such as the entrances.

Universities. Completely carpeted buildings of large institutions have carpet in classrooms, dining facilities, lounges, auditoriums, libraries, and offices. Carpet in colleges is as patchwork and varied as their architecture. As colleges have grown, wings have been added, buildings remodeled, and new buildings constructed while others have been torn down. Carpets, too, are carried over, remodeled, patched, cleaned, or newly installed.

Drew University officials said, "Ten years ago it was resilient tile. Carpet started in the offices and spread to the academic areas. Now it is everywhere, even on the walls."

When the noise from a dorm lounge was disturbing the students whose rooms adjoined it, the carpeting in the room was continued up the wall next to the bedrooms, and sound transmission was controlled to everyone's satisfaction.

Carpet is also being used on dor-mitory corridor walls to absorb some of the wear as well as control sound. This has been a very positive improvement, both practically and visually.

Rutgers University administrators related their experience with carpet that sums up carpet specifying. "Four or five years ago 40-ounce goods were specified, usually wool and then acrylic. Now it's just soil-concealing nylons that are being used. Maintenance is the key factor in the life of a carpet. Wool gives a look that cannot be achieved in nylon, but wool cannot be cleaned as easily as these nylons, except for burns."

11

Airports

The recent growth of air travel has led to a tremendous expansion of terminal facilities. New construction and renovation of existing facilities has led to a reevaluation of materials. Traditionally terrazzo has been used in areas of very heavy pedestrian traffic. But today terrazzo is giving way to carpeting and for very sound practical reasons. Carpet is proving to be an outstandingly successful floor covering for airport installations.

Terrazzo vs. Carpeting

Terrazzo is essentially a mixture of marble chips and Portland cement. The Portland cement is porous and must be sealed, and the sealer protected with wax or a wax-based cleaner. The sealer is usually stripped once or twice a year and then resealed and rewaxed. Terrazzo requires a constant maintenance program to preserve its surface. It must be mopped daily. Damp mopping, scrubbing, spot removal, and buffing are necessary to keep it from becoming discolored and abraided. It is normally considered a permanent flooring that lasts as long as the building, but it cracks readily. Repair and replacement are costly and inconvenient. The cracks, pits, and chipping that occur naturally in terrazzo are a major problem during renovations, resulting in extensive replacement that is noisy, dirty, and time consuming.

Renovation and flexible use of facilities are a prime factor in airport utility. Many changes can be anticipated during the life of the building such as expansion and rearrangement of partitions and counters. Terrazzo is not as flexible for this as carpet is.

The San Francisco Airport architects—John Carl Warnecke and Associates and Dreyfuss and Blackford—prepared a detailed analysis of carpeting and terrazzo. It included a study of maintenance costs based on costs of local maintenance firms; an evaluation of the study made by the Wharton Study Group and studies made by the American Carpet Institute; and a report from the National Terrazzo and Mosaic Association. After summarizing these various reports, the architects came out strongly for carpeting, citing all the inherent benefits of carpeting, the widespread use of carpeting in all classes of architecture, and the development of durable synthetic fibers and new installation techniques. In addition it cited the strong indications that carpeting could result in cost savings throughout the projected life of the building. The analysis of costs of carpet versus terrazzo was most persuasively in favor of the use of carpeting. The San Francisco Airport study represents an exercise in impartial cost analysis that can be considered as relevant today as it was when it was written in 1971.

Design Considerations

There are unique design problems that must be met in airport terminal carpets. Besides integration of the design with the architecture, furniture, and traffic flow, the design must also consider the following:

1. Heavy Traffic. The volume of traffic is very great. There are highly concentrated traffic lanes at entrances, concourses to boarding areas, counters, escalators, and baggage claim areas. The wear on these areas is intense, especially at pivot points. Cut piles or loose construction quickly show crushing. Areas that receive the most wear should have carpet that can be replaced easily or carpet that is of a heavier construction than what is used generally. The design for these areas can be graphically different from the general carpet and therefore aid in the flow of traffic. By making these areas read differently, color and pattern matching will not be a problem when replacements are necessary.

2. Effect of Open Areas. The physical dimensions of the vast open spaces exaggerate the defects of the floor covering. The large expanses can expose the unevenness of the slab as well as irregularities in the carpet construction. Space-dyed carpets reveal a banding and chevron effect. Banding gives the effect of a stripe running down the length of a roll of carpet. Besides being objectionable in itself, banding also emphasizes cross seaming when one set of bands stop and another appears to start. Chevroning is an effect in tweeds that sometimes becomes apparent when viewing a large section of carpet from a distance. The pattern blends into an overall irregular zigzag design These problems are worse when there is great contrast in the color of the tweeds used for the space dyes.

Carpets with linear patterns do not always run straight, and their lines become wavy or bent. This becomes exaggerated when seen over a large expanse. Seams act as a linear element and can be highly visible over a wide area. Double-heddle or staggered-stitch weaves do not seam as well as others.

3. Appearance Life. The appearance of a carpet can shorten its life before it is actually worn out. The carpet will look worn from soiling, spotting, burns, and traffic crush. The appearance level must be high.

4. Pattern. Some form of pattern is essential for long appearance life to minimize soiling, spotting, burns, and wear. A random all-over pattern is the most successful in accomplishing this goal.

Pattern can be achieved in two ways. Wilton designs offer the most sturdy and versatile carpets made. The printed tufted carpet is inexpensive, but design slippage, streaks, and blurred colors are still a problem. Axminsters could provide the necessary patterns, but they crush and show shading and wear.

5. Installation. Because of the large unbroken spaces and the use of carpet on ramps, tackless installation is not practical, and seams should be

TABLE 12. AIRPORT CARPET SPECIFICATIONS

Airport	Year	Type	Fiber	Ply	Pitch/Gauge
McCarren International Airport	1967	Wilton	Antron	4	216
Las Vegas, Nevada	1973	Tufted	Anso	3	256
Tampa International Airport	1971	Wilton	Antron	4	180
Tampa, Florida		Velvet	Antron	3	216
		Tufted[b]	Nylon	[c]	3/8 (72)
Byrd International Airport	1970	Velvet[d]	Anso	3	243
Richmond, Virginia					
Dulles International Airport	1970	Tufted	Anso	3	1/10 (270)
Washington, D.C.					
National Airlines	1970	Tufted	Anso	3	256
Kennedy International Airport					
New York					
Pan American Airlines	1972	Velvet[f]	Wool[g]	4	126
Kennedy International Airport		Velvet	Wool	3	216
New York		Velvet	Acrylic	3	216

[a]Tufts per square inch   [c]Information not available   [e].130/.150   [g]Double heddle
[b]Shag   [d]Jacquard   [f].185/.135

Rows/Stitches	Pile Height, Inches	Face Weight, Ounces	Total Weight, Ounces	Tpsi[a]
6.75	.290	32	68	54
9.5	.125	19	47	117.25
9	.230	40	75	59.4
9	.188	31.7	60.7	72
4	1 1/8	38	86	10 +
10	.130[e]	26	[c]	90
8	7/32	20	84	80
8.25	.185[e]	17.5	[c]	78 +
9	.437	60	120	50
8	.250	46.83	76.79	72
9	.250	46	77.25	81

kept to a minimum. Carpets glued down on the slab without added padding work most successfully.

Below is a study of the installations in six terminals across the country. Tables 12 and 13 show the basic specifications and other relevant information.

The six terminals have unique problems that have been solved in different ways. The experiences with each installation reinforce the observations made above. They also indicate that no single carpet specification can serve all the needs of any terminal. Such considerations are best illustrated in the Tampa Airport that comes as close to an ideal solution as anyone could wish.

TABLE 13. AIRPORT CARPET INSTALLATIONS

Airport	Year	Type
McCarren International Airport Las Vegas, Nevada	1967 1973	Wilton Tufted
Tampa International Airport Tampa, Florida	1971	Wilton Velvet Tufted
Byrd International Airport Richmond, Virginia	1970	Velvet
Dulles International Airport Washington, D.C.	1970	Tufted
National Airlines Kennedy International Airport New York	1970	Tufted
Pan American Airlines Kennedy International Airport New York	1972	Velvet Velvet Velvet

Location	Installation	Yardage	Projected Life, Years	Estimated Life, Years
Throughout	Tackless over pad	9,000 +	5	6 1/2
Throughout	Glue down	30,000 +	5	Less than 5
Large areas	Glue down	30,000 total	7	Longer than 7
Aisles	Glue down		7	Longer than 7
Islands	Glue down		7	Longer than 7
Lobby	3/16-in. vulcanized sponge rubber glue down	1,250	5–7	5
Customs	3/16-in. high-density foam rubber glue down	700	5	5
Throughout	3/16-in. fire-retardant sponge rubber glue down	10,000	5	3–5
Gate lounge	Tackless over pad	25,000 total	5–7	5
Sterile corridor	Tackless over pad		5–7	Less than 5–7
Baggage claims, Customs	Tackless over pad		5–7	1

McCarren International Airport
Las Vegas, Nevada

McCarren, the world's first carpeted airport, was a landmark installation. It was first carpeted in 1967 after the terminal had been in operation for 4 years and the original tile floors had begun to deteriorate. McCarren provides the model and inspiration for other carpeted airports around the country.

When carpet was first installed, its benefits were dramatically illustrated. The number of injury claims from spills and falls were virtually eliminated. Before installation the noise level had been so high that personnel efficiency suffered, and the public address system was indecipherable. After the carpet was installed, the noise level was lowered, and most remarkably, even around the area of slot machines the sounds are less jangling and more muted. The public reaction to the carpeting has been very enthusiastic, and the airport management could not be happier.

The original carpet was an excellent, heavy-duty Antron Wilton. It was specified by the airport under a maintenance lease contract. The maintenance company that was awarded the contract purchased the specified carpet and provided the installation and maintenance for a 5-year period. That contract has now expired. Because the airport authority was so pleased with the arrangement, they are replacing the original carpet with a newly specified one under another 5-year rental maintenance plan. After 6½ years' use, the carpet is being replaced in phases as work on the expanding facilities is completed.

The terminal building is a bustling, active area that has gone through several stages of expansion. That has meant that the original carpet not only had to take normal airport traffic, but also endure the continuous tracking in of heavy soil and dirt from the construction. The carpet color chosen was a bright, gold moresque tweed flecked with black that clearly reflects the carefree vacation atmosphere of Las Vegas. But the color could not stand up under the enormous amount of soiling tracked in at the entrances. Although gold shows more soiling than any other color, its appearance level remains good after 6½ years in the areas where tracking of soil was under control. Although the scale of the black flecks is too small to conceal cigarette burns, plugging was very successful in coping with that problem. The fiber looked worn only at the stair nosings, and the original sewn seams were in excellent condition. The carpet was installed over rubberized hair padding.

Carpeting in large areas of the main terminal lobby remains untouched from the original installation. Other areas were pieced and patched as the terminal expanded. Here color changes were apparent and showed that no thought had been given originally to allow for the problems of expansion.

In conclusion, the carpet performed well beyond its 5-year contract life in spite of the tremendous wear from construction and expansion. Its light gold color and tiny black flecks were its only limitation.

Expansion of the facilities to 3 times its original size and expiration of the carpet contract brought about new carpet specification written by Moffit and McDaniels, the airport architects. When I visited the airport, both the old and the new carpet could be seen and compared. The new carpet, in use for 3 months, was installed in two concourses to the boarding rotundas and in the two rotundas themselves. The concourses also had a special wall carpeting that extended from floor to ceiling.

The newly specified carpeting is a very dense, tufted, low-loop pile Anso nylon that is described by its manufacturer as "a board of nylon." It is in several colorations of red and blue and is glued down. The performance for 3 months would indicate that the wear life will last for the guaranteed time of 5 years offered by the fiber manufacturer. But the appearance life of the carpet may be much shorter. The carpet does not conceal surface dirt. The soil remains on top of the carpet because the pile height is so minimal and there is no concealing pattern or color. Slight color variations and streaks are visible down the carpet's length and accent cross seams.

The contrast between the old and the new carpet is very marked. The old carpet, as worn as it is after 6½ years, appears richer, warmer, quieter, and more attractive than the new one. The older carpet has all the virtues of a sturdy Wilton, and even with its drawback in color, it would out-perform the new "bargain."

Tampa International Airport
Hillsborough County Aviation Authority
Tampa, Florida

If McCarren Airport can be described as a landmark installation, then Tampa Airport can be called an exemplary model. The Hillsborough County Aviation Authority seems to have done everything right in planning one of the most successful airport complexes imaginable.

At McCarren, carpet was originally installed after the terminal had been in operation, so that the original furniture and accessories were not selected with the carpet in mind. At Tampa, the carpet was part of the original planning and part of the total concept. The criteria and design were worked out with careful study by the interior designers, Joseph Maxwell and Associates.

The airport is based on the airside/landside concept developed by the architects Reynolds, Smith and Hills. A series of airside satellites are devoted to the needs of the airplane and are connected by a passenger shuttle system to a central landside terminal that accommodates the passengers ground-based needs. The landside terminal, the shuttle cars, and three of the four airside terminals are completely carpeted. The airside terminals are tenanted by the airlines, which specified their own carpets. The landside building, in use since 1971, contains about 30,000 square yards of carpet, beautifully integrated with the architecture, traffic flow, and furniture.

There are three types of carpet, all cemented to the slab, in the landside terminal. Each is integrated with the other, and each has its own function

(Fig. 54). The major carpet is an Antron Wilton in a brown and black nonlinear pattern. The pattern is of sufficient scale and random design to effectively conceal burns and chewing gum. The general color scheme shows no soiling and is installed in blocks of individual dye lots separated by "corridors" of a contrasting related carpet in 3-foot wide bands.

The bands are the second type of carpet used. Instead of Wilton, these are Antron velvets with a conplimentary smaller-scaled pattern. These bands have several functions: they help break up the large open areas, they help direct the flow of traffic, they relate to the architecture, and they provide easily replaced traffic lanes and pivot points in front of escalators and counters (Fig. 55).

The third type of carpet is designed to be a complete contrast to the architecturally dominate major carpets. Instead of flat carpet with a neutral color scheme, the third type of carpet is an accent carpet of bright, warm colors and a soft shag surface. It is used to delineate seating areas and acts visually to break up the large spaces, providing a textural and colorful counterpoint (Fig. 56). Since the seating areas do not receive as much wear as the other areas, a less rugged carpet can be used here effectively. The shag can be easily removed for replacement if worn, without disturbing the established design.

The furniture is designed with the carpet's maintenance in mind. The seats, cantalevered from a central

pedestal, were designed with a generously large table top that has a lip so that it can contain anything that might spill on the carpet. The table top also holds a large fixed ashtray. Possible accidents that could mar the carpet are greatly minimized with these simple provisions.

Carpeting is also used at the front of the ticket counters and experimentally in the elevators, with good effect.

All these carefully worked out considerations result in a most successful terminal where all the elements contribute to its successful operation. The carpet has been planned for a life of 7 years, but it will undoubtedly last longer before repairs and replacements are needed. After 2 years it still does not need to be shampooed. That is in contrast to every other airport where shampooing is done every week or month. Daily vacuuming is all that is required, making for a very economical installation.

The enthusiastic public response to the building is in sharp contrast to that which the old terminal received. The building and the floors had been very mistreated, and it was feared that the same public would abuse the new building. But the positive overall effect of the terminal has reversed this behavior. Vandalism is practically nonexistent now, according to airport authorities.

Figure 54. (Above) Tampa International Airport's large open areas have a sense of warmth and definition. Courtesy Bigelow Carpet Co.

Figure 55. (Right) At Tampa International Airport warm incandescent lighting gives a pleasant effect to the open areas and adds to the textural quality of the carpet and other architectural materials. Courtesy Bigelow Carpet Co.

Figure 56. Tampa International Airport seating areas have shag-carpeted islands in bright warm colors. Courtesy Bigelow Carpet Co.

Richard E. Byrd International Airport
Richmond, Virginia

Expansion and renovation of busy Byrd Airport incorporated the original building as the hub of a stylized "X." It became the central waiting lounge from which passengers walk to the newly added concourses and flight gates. William Voorhees, the Director of Interior Design for Marcellus Wright Cox and Cilimberg, the airport's architects, decided to use carpeting in this area for very good reasons.

Since the original building had terrazzo floors and an integrated base, and much of the area was to be demolished, carpeting allowed less expensive patching, leveling, etc., to be done rather than trying to match the old hard-surface floors and bases. The carpeted bases act as wall bumpers for cleaning equipment, furnishings, baggage carts and the like.

Prior to the specifications and installation of carpeting, acoustics were nearly unbearable. Safety for passengers was another consideration for our decision to use carpeting in lieu of smooth floor covering.

Mr. Voorhees developed a handsome carpet design for the area with a mini-check pattern that conceals cigarette burns and soiling and coloration that coordinates with an overall scheme. The carpet combines light and dark blues and black in a neat, small-scaled grid design. A unique feature of the design is the use of a narrow selvage with a tweed texture on either side of the 54-inch wide carpet (Fig. 57). This was designed primarily to minimize the problem of matching the pattern because of the long run of the carpet and the small repeat of the design. The selvage stripes also provide an attractive camouflage for the seams. In addition, the stripe directs the flow of traffic and mirrors the pattern of exposed ceiling beams.

It is a low-loop woven carpet of Anso fiber with a 5-year wear guarantee. It has a $^3/_{16}$-inch vulcanized sponge-rubber backing that is cemented to the existing terrazzo floor and base.

The carpet has a very neat appearance and an attractive color. The pile height, density, and backing are firm enough for wheeled equipment to move smoothly. However, there are some problems caused by the sponge backing at the stairs and at the seams. At the stairs the carpet has slipped out of the nosings and come up at the treads. In the main waiting lounge, the seams are opening up even in areas away from the pressure of traffic. It has been necessary to reglue some seams after 2 years of wear, and they have not stayed closed. When I visited the airport, almost every seam had opened up in one place or another.

The cause of this problem is not easy to determine. Perhaps the cotton primary backing has shrunk from shampooing or the contraction of the rubber with age.

The design of the carpet, while very attractive, does not solve the problems of carpeting large open spaces. The small scale of the pattern shows irregularities in the weave when they occur occasionally, and it does not conceal burns and soiling as well as a larger, more random pattern would. Soiling is a problem in this airport as the ash urns are easily overturned, and the water in the urns stains the carpet.

The carpet is also used behind the airline ticket counters. The regular maintenance service is not used here, and the airlines have an outside janitorial service that cares for it. This is an area of concentrated use, with a lot of pivoting that gives the area the hardest kind of wear. Unfortunately, the carpet cannot take it. It was crushed and worn, showing a great deal of abrasion after 3 years of wear.

Figure 57. *The carpet in the Byrd International Airport lobby has a light blue stripe that is actually the selvage of each carpet strip; it was so designed to make it easier to install. Courtesy Allied Chemical Corp., Anso nylon fiber.*

Dulles International Airport
Washington, D.C.

A bright red carpet welcomes deplaning passengers at the International Arrivals area and Customs Inspection Section of Dulles (Fig. 58) that was renovated and expanded to twice its original size in 1970. This area contains the first use of carpet in the handsome airport.

Deplaning passengers from international flights who must pass customs inspection are usually tired, restless, and noisy. Carpeting successfully serves to put them more at their ease, quiet the excited sounds, and cushion the bottles of liquor or perfume that inevitably fall (Fig. 59). Airport authorities are so delighted with the carpet's performance that they would like to see more carpet used in the future.

The carpet is a low, dense, tufted loop of Anso with a 5-year wear guarantee. It is bonded to a ³/₁₆-inch thick, high-density foam back that is cemented directly to the floor. The carpet generally presents an attractive appearance because of its very cheerful coloration—a bright red space-dyed tweed. The problems that sometimes occur with space-dyed carpets are not present here. The color is not streaky, and it all appears to be from the same dye lot. There is no concealing pattern to hide burns, but the airport staff seems to keep up with the problem

by successful and inconspicuous plugging. Seams are not a problem.

This carpet bears comparison with the newly installed carpet at McCarren and the cushioned carpet at Byrd. The Dulles carpet has fewer tufts per square inch and a slightly higher pile, so it is less dense than that at McCarren and gives greater concealment to surface soil and dust. Its density will not affect its wear as it has sufficient face weight. Seams are less conspicuous at Dulles than at McCarren, perhaps because of the slightly higher pile. Although both the Dulles carpet and the Byrd carpet have attached cushions and both were installed in 1970, the seams at Byrd have become an increasing problem, pulling apart for a reason that cannot be determined. At Byrd the 54-inch carpet is vulcanized to ³/₁₆-inch sponge rubber that the manufacturer claims will last longer than the carpet. At Dulles the carpet is bonded to ³/₁₆-inch high-density foam rubber that has taken the same amount of traffic wear and shampooing as that at Byrd, but the seams have not opened up. The difference could be in the quality of installation, the performance of sponge (Byrd) as compared with foam (Dulles), or shrinking of the backing from shampooing.

Figure 58. At Dulles International Airport all passengers disembarking from international flights arrive at this point and continue down a ramp to the customs area. Courtesy Allied Chemical Corp., Anso nylon fiber.

Figure 59. The Dulles International Airport customs area. Courtesy Allied Chemical Corp., Anso nylon fiber.

National Airlines Passenger Terminal
Kennedy International Airport
New York, N.Y.

Except for the travertine floor on the street level, carpeting is used throughout the handsome terminal that I. M. Pei and Partners designed for National Airlines. Open since 1970, the terminal used a standard carpet in a custom color that is a stock-dyed, low-loop tufted pile of Anso with a 5-year wear guarantee. It is bonded to a $\frac{3}{16}$-inch sponge rubber, fire-retardant backing guaranteed by Goodrich for the life of the carpet, and it is glued down. There is no pattern and only a very slight texture.

The carpet is used over the entire mezzanine waiting area, which is a large, unbroken expanse, and through a bridge that leads to the carpeted satellites and ramps. All passenger traffic is funneled through the bridge.

The color of the carpet is its chief asset as well as one of its drawbacks. The strong red color makes a vigorous statement flowing through the spaces and holding its own as a strong, flat plane. At night the building glows with rosy reflected light from the carpet, warming and coloring the architectural space from both inside and out. The large glass expanse that characterizes the building exposes the carpeting to strong sunlight, and as a result, the manufacturer would not guarantee the colorfastness. After less than 3 years the color has conspicuously faded from the sun. Patches made in the carpet in these spots to plug burns look conspicuous because there is a difference in color between the older carpet and the new plug. Fortunately, there are not too many of these spots.

Cigarette scarring is a problem in areas around the many telephone kiosks, which are heavily used, but where there are either not enough ash trays or none at all. Besides showing burns, the carpet is compressed, worn, and discolored in these areas. Other areas of concentrated use like the stairways and the bridge also show extensive compression and wear despite the guarantee. It would appear that the face weight of 17.5 ounces is not adequate for the traffic.

The light from the large windows reveals irregularities in the slab that are reflected in the carpet. In one area the carpet looked so lumpy that only after the carpet was lifted to check the problem was it proven to be a fault of the spawling concrete.

Delamination is apparent from the lumps and ripples that appear in the carpet behind a counter where all passenger tickets are closed out. The carpet appears loose and buckled, and is without doubt separated from its backing. This delamination is the result of concentrated pivoting and twisting as the people working at the small counter in a constricted space constantly move back and forth. Except for that area, the bonded sponge-rubber backing appears to be performing well. The carpet is supportive underfoot, and wheeled carts and wheelchairs move easily. Seams are invisible, and unlike Byrd airport, there is no shrinkage to open the seams.

There are several instances of pulled threads on the stairs, which can be a serious problem with tufted carpets. The manufacturer claimed a tuft bind of 15 pounds for this carpet, which obviously was not sufficient.

In spite of the problems noted, the overall appearance of the carpet remains good.

Pan American Airlines Passenger Terminal
Kennedy International Airport
New York, N.Y.

The expansion of Pan American's facilities at Kennedy Airport brought together top architects, a famous design firm, and a carpet consultant. Architects Tippets, Abbot and MacCarthy (TAM) hired Elliot Noyes and Associates for the interiors; and for the specification writing Elliot Noyes consulted with Al Caputo of Gotham Carpets who worked with the mills and developed samples. It was to be a quality installation, with half a million dollars' worth of carpeting. But nothing went the way it was planned. Some of the carpeting must be replaced after only 1 year.

Three different carpet specifications were called for. A rich, double-heddle, thick wool loop pile is used in the gate lounges (Fig. 60). A lower pile, lighter-weight wool carpet, with a cut and uncut pile, was used in the sterile corridors, and an acrylic was installed in the customs area (Fig. 61) as well as in the baggage claims area. This carpet was originally planned to be an Antron carpet, but that was not available in time for installation and Acrylan was a last-minute substitution. The designer chose wool for its fire-retardant qualities and cleanability, and by using standard running lines the flammability ratings were assured.

One of the designer's basic decisions was to have a soft feeling underfoot, so the carpet was installed over a pad in all the carpeted areas. This was done to mark the transition from the vast uncarpeted terrazzo floor flowing through most of the terminal. The designer wanted the feeling of moving from a very hard floor to a very soft floor.

Problems developed right away. Installers working under poor conditions had to lay sections of carpet in a hot, humid period before the building's humidity control was operating. The pad was glued to the slab, and the carpet started shifting over it, buckling and rippling. It had to be restretched, but ripples are still present as the carpet shifts over the large expanses.

The carpet and pad in the customs and baggage claim areas have caused the most dissatisfaction. The carpet cushion makes it very hard to wheel baggage carts around, and when these carts are loaded with the many bags that a family takes on vacation, the pressure on the carpet of pushing and pulling causes buckling. The scarring from cigarette burns is impossible to keep pace with since there are an inadequate number of ash trays and there is no pattern in the carpet to hide the burns. After 1 year's use, the carpet and pad in this area are scheduled to be replaced with new Antron carpet that will be glued to the slab, which should take care of the rippling and future wear. But it will be interesting to see how the scarring problem is handled.

Another basic decision that was to have its effect was the stripe the designer specified in the carpets for the gate lounges, customs, and baggage claims areas. The designer wanted a "controlled geometry," but wanted to avoid a "salt and pepper look." He achieved a neat stripe that is used in various colorations to differentiate gate lounges. But the stripe emphasizes floor irregularities and carpet ripples and spotlights seams when the stripes do not match or run true. Because the stripes make burn patching a problem on the acrylic carpet, the cookie-cutter technique cannot be easily applied since the patches must carefully line up with the stripes.

An additional problem is that the seams are conspicuous in the gate lounge carpets, even when the stripes do not highlight them, because of the double-heddle carpet construction and workmanship of the installation.

The carpet where the most concentrated flow of traffic occurs—in the sterile corridors where deplaning passengers are confined on their way to the customs area—is showing wear. The carpet here is less dense and has a lighter face weight than the gate lounge carpet. It also has a cut and uncut loop that makes a plaid pattern. The cut pile has crushed and shaded considerably under the pressure of the traffic, and there are discoloration and wear at the pivot points where the traffic turns corners.

In 1972, the 25,000 yards of carpet were projected to have a life of 5 years. The customs area will not survive its first year, and the sterile corridors may look worn out soon after.

Figure 60. The Pan American
Airlines Terminal gate lounges
at Kennedy International Airport.
Courtesy Pan American Airlines.

12

Offices
and
Banks

The following survey of installations shows typical conditions of wear and maintenance. Except for all the Chase Manhattan Bank carpets, all other carpets discussed are readily available in the manufacturers' standard running lines.

Included in this survey are several fibers and constructions. There are two glued-down installations, two carpets that use the unusual combination of 70 percent acrylic– 30 percent nylon. There are three "Millstar" installations with the same blend. ("Millstar" is not discussed elsewhere in this book; however, these installations were made available for inspection and because of the general interest in the material, they are included.)

Carpet in offices and banks does not have the same degree of restrictions and criteria for performance as carpet in public places does. The social and environmental impact is lessened, which means that businesses can indulge themselves. They can replace their carpeting as often as they wish to present an image that serves their purpose—from utilitarian to ultra luxury. But all carpet is selected with an ideal image of how it should perform.

How does the reality measure up to the ideal? Draw your own conclusions based on this small but typical sampling of office and bank installations.

Bulova Watch Company
630 Fifth Ave.
New York City

General Office and Corridors.
Carpet down 5 years. Beige loop pile looks very good after a long period of wear. There is slight pile crush and surface wear, as would be expected.

Weave	Velvet
Pitch	216
Rows	8
Pile ht.	.250
Yarn	Wool
Ply	3
Face wt.	46.

Chase Manhattan Bank
1 New York Plaza
New York City

Cafeteria. Small, checked carpet in blue down 2 years. Receives very heavy use. Watermarked but not worn.

Weave	Axminster
Pitch	189
Rows	9
Pile ht.	27/32
Yarn	Wool
Ply	3
Face wt.	51.9
Total wt.	92.6

General Offices. Same small checked carpet in beiges and brown down 2 years. Designed to conceal coffee stains and burns. Watermarked.

Club Lounges. Two lounges, one in yellow cut pile, the other in green cut pile. Pile shows traffic lanes and wear patterns, making carpet look worn even though it is a rich, thick pile.

Weave	Velvet
Pitch	216
Rows	9½
Pile ht.	.500
Yarn	Wool
Ply	3

Face wt.	81.7
Total wt.	118.2

Large Interior Back Shop Area.
Red and dark-red stripe of cut and uncut pile. Low, tight construction. Carpet is soiled and color dimmed from wear after 1 year. No chair pads necessary. No pile crush. Carpet is tracked from entrance doors through traffic lanes. *Note*: This carpet had Brunslon added. All other carpets are treated for static control at regular intervals.

Weave	Velvet
Pitch	216
Rows	8
Pile ht.	.205 cut .250 uncut
Yarn	30% nylon–70% acrylic
Ply	3
Face wt.	69.8
Total wt.	95.3

Chemical Bank
277 Park Ave.
New York City

Back Shop Areas. Carpet down 4 months. Glued down with release cement. Owner reports that access to underfloor ducts works well. Light color shows dulling and spotting. Traffic lanes are dark. Tight, low loop does not crush. No chair pads used. *Note*: Brunslon added to carpet.

Weave	Velvet
Pitch	216
Rows	8
Pile ht.	.200
Yarn	30% nylon– 70% acrylic
Ply	4
Face wt.	51.
Total wt.	81.

J. K. Lasser
666 Fifth Ave.
New York City

General Offices and Corridors. Carpet down 2½ years. Light gray in corridors, tan in offices. Generally good appearance. Shows slight pile compression in corridors. Seams good.

Weave	Tufted
Gauge	⅛
Stitches	6
Pile ht.	9/32
Yarn	Wool
Ply	3
Face wt.	41.
Total wt.	79.

Marsteller, Inc.
866 Third Ave.
New York City

General Offices, Corridors, and Elevators. Carpet down 3 years. Looks old and worn although it is just crushed and soiled. Wax from tiled areas is ruining its appearance. Pile is too soft for heavy traffic at elevators. Traffic lanes are very worn.

Weave	Velvet
Pitch	216
Rows	7
Pile ht.	.368
Yarn	Wool
Ply	6
Face wt.	52.

Metropolitan Life Insurance Company
1 Madison Ave.
New York City

Three Small Offices. Carpet tiles down 8 to 9 months. Tiles adhere to floor well. One office, in blue, receives more traffic, and the tiles have blended into each other well. Traffic lanes are apparent. Two offices in copper color look more soiled even though less used.

Carpet	"Millstar"
Yarn	30% nylon—70% acrylic

Milliken Corporate Headquarters
1045 Sixth Ave.
New York City

Cafeteria. Carpet tiles down 1 year. Tiles are rotated to conceal wear. Color choice, dark gray, important in concealing soil. Appearance is flat but acceptable.

Carpet	"Millstar"
Yarn	30% nylon—70% acrylic

Private, Dining Room. Carpet down 1 year over pad. Seams are fair. Color choice, copper, shows soiling and traffic lanes. Cigarette burns are conspicuous.

Reavis and McGrath
1 Chase Manhattan Plaza
New York City

General Offices and Corridors. Coffee-brown tweed carpet down 3 months. It was installed over existing carpet. Seams poor. Shows pile crush in traffic lanes. Heavy shedding and fuzzing. Very luxurious appearance marred by these defects.

Weave	Tufted
Gauge	⅛
Stitches	5
Pile ht.	⅜
Yarn	30% modacrylic—70% acrylic
Ply	4
Face wt.	64
Total wt.	102

**Texaco
Chrysler Building
Lexington Ave.
New York City**

General Office. Carpet down 6 months. Permanently glued down. Owner voiced regret about no easy access to underfloor ducts. Slight pile crush at entrance to room. No chair pads used. White circle formed under swivel chairs from unknown cause. Slight pile crush at swivel chairs. Burnt orange color and appearance good.

Weave	Tufted
Gauge	⅛
Stitches	8.1
Pile ht.	.190
Yarn	Antron II
Ply	4
Face wt.	26.2
Total wt.	60.2

**Union Dime Savings Bank
39 Street and Madison Ave.
New York City**

Street Banking Floor. Carpet down 2½ years. Red and green plaid effect, with 12 rows cut and 12 rows uncut. Carpet watermarked immediately after installation; gives a very unsatisfactory appearance. Pile reversal and surface crush accented at pivot points. Owner very unhappy.

Weave	Velvet
Pitch	216
Rows	8
Pile ht.	.250
Yarn	Wool
Ply	4
Face wt.	72

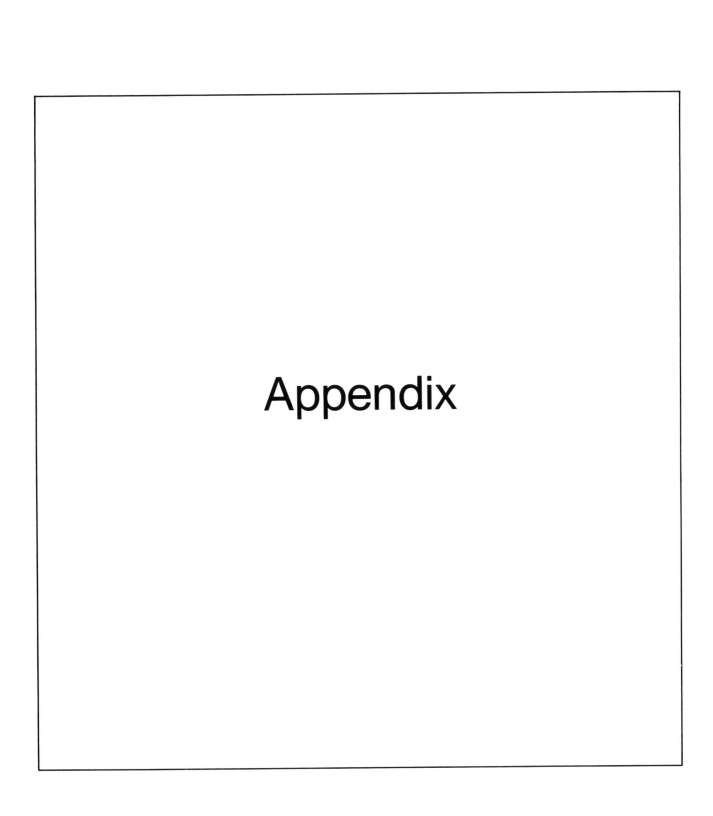

Appendix

TABLE A. SOME PHYSICAL PROPERTIES OF MAN-MADE FIBERS

Fiber[a]	Breaking Tenacity[b] Grams per denier		Specific Gravity[c]	Standard Moisture Regain, %[d]	Effects of Heat
	Standard	Wet			
ACETATE					
Filament and Staple	1.2–1.5	.8–1.2	1.32	6.0	Sticks at 350°–375°F. Softens at 400°–445°F. Melts at 500°F. Burns relatively slowly.
ACRYLIC					
Filament and Staple	2.0–3.5	1.8–3.3	1.14–1.19	1.3–2.5	Sticks at 450°–497°F, depending on type.
ARAMID					
High Tenacity Resistant: Filament	4.8–5.8	3.8–4.8	1.38	5	Decomposes above 700°F.
Staple	3.0–4.0	2.0–3.0	1.38	5	Decomposes above 700°F.
MODACRYLIC					
Filament and Staple	2.0–3.5	2.0–3.5	1.30–1.37	.4–4.0	Will not support combustion. Shrinks at 250°F. Stiffens at temperatures over 300°F.

[a]Standard laboratory conditions for fiber tests: 70°F and 65 percent relative humidity.

[b]Breaking tenacity: the stress at which a fiber breaks.

[c]Specific gravity: the ratio of the weight of a given volume of fiber to an equal volume of water.

[d]Standard moisture regain: The moisture regain of a fiber (expressed as a percentage of the moisture-free weight) at 70°F and 65 percent relative humidity.

[e]Depending on type.

Note: Data given in ranges may fluctuate according to introduction of fiber modifications or additions and deletions of fiber types.

Courtesy Man-Made Fiber Producers Association, Inc.

Fiber[a]	Breaking Tenacity[b] Grams per denier		Specific Gravity[c]	Standard Moisture Regain, %[d]	Effects of Heat
	Standard	Wet			
NYLON					
Nylon 66 Regular Tenacity Filament	3.0–6.0	2.6–5.4	1.14	4.0–4.5	Sticks at 445°F. Melts at about 500°F.
Nylon 66 High Tenacity Filament	6.0–9.5	5.0–8.0	1.14	4.0–4.5	Same as above.
Nylon 66, Staple	3.5–7.2	3.2–6.5	1.14	4.0–4.5	Same as above.
Nylon 6, Filament	6.0–9.5	5.0–8.0	1.14	4.5	Melts at 414°–428°F.
Nylon 6, Staple	2.5	2.0	1.14	4.5	Melts at 414°–428°F.
OLEFIN (Polypropylene)					
Filament and Staple	4.8–7.0	4.8–7.0	.91		Melts at 325°–335°F.
POLYESTER					
Regular Tenacity Filament	4.0–5.0	4.0–5.0	1.22 or 1.38[e]	.4 or .8[e]	Melts at 480°–550°F.
High Tenacity Filament	6.3–9.5	6.2–9.4	1.22 or 1.38[e]	.4 or .8[e]	Melts at 480°–550°F.
Regular Tenacity Staple	2.5–5.0	2.5–5.0	1.22 or 1.38[e]	.4 or .8[e]	Melts at 480°–550°F.
High Tenacity Staple	5.0–6.5	5.0–6.4	1.22 or 1.38[e]	.4 or .8[e]	Melts at 480°–550°F.
RAYON					
Filament and Staple					
Regular Tenacity	.73–2.6	.7–1.8	1.50–1.53	13	Does not melt. Decomposes at 350°–464°F.
Medium Tenacity	2.40–3.2	1.2–1.9	1.50–1.53	13	Burns readily.
High Tenacity	3.00–6.0	1.9–4.6	1.50–1.53	13	
High Wet Modulus	2.50–5.5	1.8–4.0	1.50–1.53	13	
SPANDEX					
Filament	.6–.9	.6–.9	1.20–1.21	.75–1.3	Degrades slowly at temperatures over 300°F. Melts at 446°–518°F.
TRIACETATE					
Filament and Staple	1.2–1.4	.8–1.0	1.3	3.2	Before heat treatment, sticks at 350°–375°F. After treatment, above 464°F. Melts at 575°F.

Pursuant to the provisions of Section 7(c) of the act, the following generic names for manufactured fibers, together with their respective definitions, are hereby established:

(a) **acrylic**—a manufactured fiber in which the fiber-forming substance is any long-chain synthetic polymer composed of at least 85% by weight of acrylonitrile units

$$(-CH_2-CH-).$$
$$|$$
$$CN$$

(b) **modacrylic**—a manufactured fiber in which the fiber-forming substance is any long-chain synthetic polymer composed of less than 85% but at least 35% by weight of acrylonitrile units,

$$(-CH_2-CH-),$$
$$|$$
$$CN$$

except fibers qualifying under subparagraph (2) of paragraph (j) of this section and fibers qualifying under paragraph (q) of this section.

(c) **polyester**—a manufactured fiber in which the fiber-forming substance is any long-chain synthetic polymer composed of at least 85% by weight of an ester of a substituted aromatic carboxylic acid, including but not restricted to substituted therephthalate units,

$$p(-R-O-C-C_6H_4-C-O-)$$
$$||\qquad\qquad ||$$
$$O\qquad\qquad O$$

and parasubstituted hydroxy-benzoate units,

$$p(-R-O-C_6H_4-C-O-).$$
$$||$$
$$O$$

(d) **rayon**—a manufactured fiber composed of regenerated cellulose, as well as manufactured fibers composed of regenerated cellulose in which substituents have replaced not more than 15% of the hydrogens of the hydroxyl groups.

(e) **acetate**—a manufactured fiber in which the fiber-forming substance is cellulose acetate. Where not less than 92% of the hydroxyl groups are acetylated, the term triacetate may be used as a generic description of the fiber.

(f) **saran**—a manufactured fiber in which the fiber-forming substance is any long-chain synthetic polymer composed of at least 80% by weight of vinylidene chloride units

$$(-CH_2-CCl_2-).$$

(g) **azlon**—a manufactured fiber in which the fiber-forming substance is composed of any regenerated naturally occurring proteins.

(h) **nytril**—a manufactured fiber containing at least 85% of a long-chain polymer of vinylidene dinitrile

$$(-CH_2-C(CN)_2-)$$

where the vinylidene dinitrile content is no less than every other unit in the polymer chain.

(i) **nylon**—a manufactured fiber in which the fiber-forming substance is a long-chain synthetic polyamide in which less than 85% of the amide

$$(-C-NH-)$$
$$||$$
$$O$$

linkages are attached directly to two aromatic rings.

(j) **rubber**—a manufactured fiber in which the fiber-forming substance is comprised of natural or synthetic rubber, including the following categories:

(1) a manufactured fiber in which the fiber-forming substance is a hydrocarbon such as natural rubber, polyisoprene, polybutadiene, copolymers of dienes and hydrocarbons, or amorphous (noncrystalline) polyolefins.

(2) a manufactured fiber in which the fiber-forming substance is a copolymer of acrylonitrile and a diene (such as butadiene) composed of not more than 50% but at least 10% by weight of acrylonitrile units.

$$(CH_2-CH-).$$
$$|$$
$$CN\cdot$$

The term "lastrile" may be used as a generic description for fibers falling within this category.

(3) a manufactured fiber in which the fiber-forming substance is a polychloroprene or a copolymer of chloroprene in which at least 35% by weight of the fiber-forming sub-

*Federal Trade Commission Rules and Regulations under the Textile Products Identification Act, as amended Sept. 12, 1973.

stance is composed of chloroprene units.

$$(-CH_2-\underset{\underset{C}{|}}{C}=CH-CH_2-).$$

(k) **spandex**—a manufactured fiber in which the fiber-forming substance is a long-chain synthetic polymer comprised of at least 85% of a segmented polyurethane.

(l) **vinal**—a manufactured fiber in which the fiber-forming substance is any long-chain synthetic polymer composed of at least 50% by weight of vinyl alcohol units

$$(C-CH_2-CHOH-)$$

and in which the total of the vinyl alcohol units and any one or more of the various acetal units is at least 85% by weight of the fiber.

(m) **olefin**—a manufactured fiber in which the fiber-forming substance is any long-chain synthetic polymer composed of at least 85% by weight of ethylene, propylene, or other olefin units, except amorphous (noncrystalline) polyolefins qualifying under category (1) of Paragraph (j) of Rule 7.

(n) **vinyon**—a manufactured fiber in which the fiber-forming substance is any long-chain synthetic polymer composed of at least 85% by weight of vinyl chloride units.

$$(-CH_2-CHCl-).$$

(o) **metallic**—a manufactured fiber composed of metal, plastic-coated metal, metal-coated plastic, or a core completely covered by metal.

(p) **glass**—a manufactured fiber in which the fiber-forming substance is glass.

(q) **anidex**—a manufactured fiber in which the fiber-forming substance is any long-chain synthetic polymer composed of at least 50% by weight of one or more esters of a monohydric alcohol and acrylic acid.

$$(CH_2=CH-COOH).$$

(r) **aramid**—a manufactured fiber in which the fiber-forming substance is a long-chain synthetic polyamide in which at least 85% of the amide

$$(\;\underset{\underset{O}{\|}}{C}\;\;NH\;)$$

linkages are attached directly to two aromatic rings.

Courtesy Man-Made Fiber Producers Association, Inc.

TABLE C. FIBERS USED IN CARPET MANUFACTURING

GENERIC TERM	ACRYLIC	MODACRYLIC	NYLON	OLEFIN (Polypropylene)	POLYESTER	WOOL
DEFINITION	Fiber-forming substance is any long chain synthetic polymer composed of at least 85% by weight of acrylonitrile units.	Fiber in which fiber-forming substance is any long chain synthetic polymer composed of less than 85% but at least 35% by wt. of acrylonitrile units.	Fiber-forming substance is any long chain synthetic polyamide having recurring amide groups as an integral part of the polymer chain.	Fiber in which fiber-forming substance is any long chain synthetic polymer composed of at least 85% by wt. of ethylene, propylene or other olefin units.	Fiber in which fiber-forming substance is any long chain synthetic polymer composed of at least 85% by wt. of an ester of a dihydric alcohol and terephthalic acid.	Fiber in which amino acids units are combined into peptide chains possessing multi dimensional stability resulting from hydrogen bonding and cross linking forces of cystine molecules through their sulfur bonds.
MANUFACTURERS	American Cyanamid Dow Badische Du Pont Monsanto	Eastman Union Carbide Monsanto	Allied Chemical (also makes a polyamide/polyester biconstituent fiber for carpet yarns) American Enka Beaunit Celanese Dow Badische Du Pont Firestone Hanover Monsanto Nylon Engineering Rohm & Haas Wellman, Inc.	(Includes face yarn and/or woven or spun bonded backing) ACS Industries Armstrong Bemis CAMAC Chevron Collins & Aik. Du Pont Enjay Fibron Hercules Moultrie Osterneck Patchogue-Plymouth Phillips Poly-Fibers Satterwhite Shuford Synthetic Indus. Tenn. Fibers Thiokol Wellington	American Enka American Viscose Beaunit Celanese Dow Badische Du Pont Eastman Hoechst Monsanto Wellman	Supplied by growers, New Zealand, Great Britain, Near East, South America, India, China.
STANDARD MOISTURE REGAIN (%)	1.3 to 2.5	.4 to 4	4 to 4.5	-8-	.4 to .8	
EFFECTS OF HEAT	420-490°F. sticking Temperature	275-300°F. sticking temperature	Sticks 320-375°F. Melts 425°F.	Melts 250-333°F.	Sticks 445-455°F. Melts 482-554°F.	Scorches at 400F., chars at 572°F.
SPECIFIC GRAVITY	1.16 to 1.18	1.31 to 1.37	1.14	0.90 to 0.96	1.38	1.30
EFFECTS OF ACIDS, ALKALIS AND SOLVENTS	Generally good resistance to mineral acids. Fair to good resistance to weak cold alkalis. Good resistance to common solvents.	Excellent resistance to highly concentrated acids. Unaffected by alkalis. Soluble in warm acetone.	Resistant to weak acids but decomposes in strong mineral acids. Alkalis have little or no effect. Soluble in phenol and formic acid.	Excellent resistance to most acids and alkalis. Generally soluble above 160°F. in chlorinated hydrocarbons.	Good to excellent resistance to mineral acids. Some affected by concentrated sulphuric acid. Decomposes in alkalis at the boil. Generally insoluble in common solvents but soluble in some phenolic compounds.	Uneffected by mineral acids. Generally good resistance to weak cold alkalis. Resistance to organic solvents.
DYESTUFFS USED	Acid, basic cationic, chrome, direct, disperse, napthol, neutral premetallized and sulphur. Some fibers are solution dyed.	Basic, cationic, disperse, neutral premetallized and vat.	Acid, direct, disperse and premetallized. Some fibers are now solution dyed.	Usually pigmented before extrusion. When modified can be dyed with selected dyestuffs.	Cationic, developed and disperse.	Acid, premetallized, fiber reactant, chrome vats and direct.
RESISTANCE TO MILDEW, AGING, SUNLIGHT AND ABRASION	Excellent resistance to mildew and aging and generally good resistance to sunlight and abrasion.	Not attacked by mildew. Good resistance to abrasion, sunlight and aging but some loss in tensile strength may be noted in the case of Dynel upon prolonged exposure to sunlight.	Excellent resistance to mildew, aging and abrasion. Some degradation may result from prolonged exposure to sunlight.	Not attacked by mildew. Good resistance to aging, abrasion and indirect sunlight. Can be stabilized to give good resistance to direct sunlight.	Excellent resistance to mildew, aging, and abrasion. In some instance prolonged exposure to sunlight will result in some loss of strength.	Generally excellent resistance to aging and abrasion. Good fastness to sunlight and mildew.

TABLE D. FIBER TRADE NAMES IN CARPET

Trade Name	Generic Class	Company Name	Type	Special Properties, Use
Acrilan +	Acrylic	Monsanto	Staple	Flame Retardant Series
Acrilan +	Acrylic	Monsanto	Staple	Flame Retardant Series
Acrilan 2000 +	Acrylic	Monsanto	Staple	Superior Colorfastness
Anavor	Polyester	Dow Badische	Fil & Staple	Bright colors, washability
Anso	Nylon	Allied Chem.	BCF, Staple	Anti-soil
Anso X	Nylon	Allied Chem.	BCF & Staple	Anti-stat
Antron	Nylon	Du Pont	BCF & Staple	Soil Hiding, newness retention
Avlin	Polyester	Amer. Viscose Div. FMC Corp.	Staple	Low static, easy cleaning
Banlon	Nylon, Polyester	Beaunit	BCF, Staple	
Brunslon	Metal/Nylon	Brunswick Corp.	Spun Yarn	Static control
Brunsmet	Metal	Brunswick Corp.	Tow	Static control
Cadon	Nylon	Monsanto	Staple & Fil.	Anti-stat
Camalon	Nylon	Camac Corp.	BCF	Sol. dyed, anti-stat, anti-soil, fade resist.
Caprolan	Nylon	Allied Chem.	BCF	
Celanese Nylon	Nylon	Celanese	BCF, Staple	
Chromeflex	Metallic	Metal Film Co.	Filament	
Creslan Acrylic	Acrylic	Amer. Cyanamid	Staple	Range of Types
Cumuloft	Nylon	Monsanto	Filament	
Dacron	Polyester	Du Pont	Staple	
Dacron III	Polyester	Du Pont	Staple	Contract market
Dynel	Modacrylic	Union Carbide	Indus. Multifil.	Flame, soil resistant
Encron	Polyester	Amer. Enka	Staple	Round and multilobal, high bulk, luster, color clarity, differential dyeing
Encron MCS	Polyester	Amer. Enka	Staple	Multilobal, differential dyeing, high bulk and luster, color clarity
Enka	Nylon or Polyester	Amer. Enka	BCF, Staple	Multilobal, piece, space differential, sparkle, cationic dyeing; soil hiding
Enkaloft	Nylon	Amer. Enka	BCF, Staple	Multilobal, piece, space differential, cationic and sparkle dyeing types
Enkalure	Nylon	Amer. Enka	BCF, Staple	Multilobal, high bulk, cover, luster, color clarity, soil hiding, 5-year wear guarantee
Enkalure II	Nylon	Amer. Enka	BCF, Staple	Same as above, superior soil hiding
Fairtex	Metallic	Riegel Paper	Monofil	Anti-stat
Fortrel	Polyester	Celanese	Staple	
Herculon	Olefin	Hercules	BCF & Staple	Ultra low static, soil resist
Hud Stat	Copper	Hudson Wire	Fil. Wire	Anti-static
Kodel	Polyester	Eastman	Staple (15D/F)	Regular, cationic, light dyeable; reg., med. bright luster
Kodel 211	Polyester	Eastman	Staple (6D/F)	For scatter rugs
Kynol	CA-0001	Carborundum	Staple	Flame resistant
Marvess	Olefin	Phillips Fibers	Staple & BCF	
Melton	Metallic	Metlon Corp.	Filament	
Mocomilon	Nylon, Polyester, Acrylics, Olefin	Moultrie Textiles, Div. Moultrie Cotton Mills	Staple	Blended anti-static fibers
Nomex	Nylon	Du Pont	Staple	Flame retardant, low smoke generation
Nyloft	Nylon	Firestone	BCF & Staple	
Orlon	Acrylic	Du Pont	Staple	
Osterlon	Polypropylene	Osterneck	Monofil	Chemical resistant
Phillips 66 Nylon	Nylon	Phillips	BCF	
Polyloom I	Polypropylene	Chevron Chem.	Fibrillated film	Soil & chemical resistant
Polyloom II	Polypropylene	Chevron Chem.	Fibrillated film	Guar. against UV
Skyloft	Rayon	Amer. Enka	BCF	Acid, differential and mock twist dyeing types
Source	Matrix/Fibril	Allied Chem.	BCF & Staple	
Sunlon	Nylon	Nylon Engineering	BCF & Staple	Solution dyed, fade, soil resist
Super Bulk	Nylon	Amer. Enka	BCF	High bulk, heatset, 2-ply in cationic, deep, light & differential dye types
Trevira	Polyester	Hoechst Fibers	Staple	Type 820, disperse dye. Type 830, deep dye. Type 840, cationic dyeable
Vectra	Polypropylene	Vectra Corp.	Staple, Fil BCF	Chemical, stain resistant, ultra low static
Verel 11A	Modacrylic	Eastman	Staple (8D/F)	For scatter rugs
Verel 16E	Modacrylic	Eastman	Staple (16D/F)	Regular, carpet
Vivana	Nylon	Dow Badische	Bulk Cont. Fil.	Wear resistance, easy dyeability, luster
Wellene	Polyester	Wellman	Staple	
Wellon	Nylon	Wellman	Staple	
Wellstrand	Nylon & Polyester	Wellman	Staple	Heavy deniers 60-80-100-200
X-Static	Nylon	Rohm & Haas	BCF, Monofil	Anti-static
Zefran	Acrylic	Dow Badische	Staple	Type A403, producer colored Type A253, basic dyeable
Zefran	Nylon	Dow Badische	BCF, Staple	Wear resistant, soil hiding, static controlled
Zefran	Blend ZK3	Dow Badische	Acrylic Modacrylic	Spun yarn in heathers and moresques, static controlled
Zefran	Blend CR4	Dow Badische	Acrylic Nylon	Spun yarns, wear resistant, static controlled
Zefstat	Metallic	Dow Badische	Ribbon	Permanent anti-static

TABLE E. MINIMUM SPECIFICATION REQUIREMENTS BASED ON PILE DENSITY FOR WOOL OR ACRYLIC CARPET

	Average Heavy Traffic		Average Medium Traffic	
	Minimum Weight per Square Yard,	Average Pile Height,	Minimum Weight per Square Yard,	Average Pile Height,
	Ounces	Inches	Ounces	Inches
Axminster Carpet	36	.200–.310	28	.200–.310
Knitted Carpet	42	.250–.300	36	.200–.250
Tufted Carpet	42	.250–.300	36	.200–.250
Velvet Carpet:				
Woven through the back	42	.200–.250	32	.175–.230
Not woven through the back	36	.200–.250	28	.175–.230
"Twist"			42	
Wilton Carpet	42	.200–.250	34	.200–.250

Courtesy American Hotel and Motel Association.

TABLE F. MINIMUM SPECIFICATION REQUIREMENTS BASED ON PILE DENSITY FOR NYLON OR POLYPROPYLENE CARPETS

	Average Heavy Traffic		Average Medium Traffic	
	Minimum Weight per Square Yard,	Average Pile Height,	Minimum Weight per Square Yard,	Average Pile Height,
	Ounces	Inches	Ounces	Inches
Tufted Carpet	28	.190–.290	22	.190–.290
Velvet Carpet Woven through the back	28	.210–.290	22	.210–.290
Loomed Carpet*	16	.150 max.		

Sponge-bonded, high-density nylon pile.

Courtesy American Hotel and Motel Association.

TABLE G. BUILDING AREAS CLASSIFIED BY EXPECTED FOOT TRAFFIC

Applications	Average Heavy Traffic	Average Medium Traffic
Office Buildings	Reception areas, aisles, open work areas, stairways, and elevators	Executive offices
Banks/Stores	Entranceways, lobbies, stairways, elevators, aisles, and selling areas*	Executive offices, semiprivate office areas, aisles, and selling areas*
Churches/Funeral Homes		Entranceways, stairways, aisles, areas under seats or benches, chapel and altar
Restaurants/Clubs	Dining areas, bars, and grill	
Schools	Corridors, classrooms, libraries, and stairways	Administrative offices and faculty lounges
Transportation: planes, trains, railroads, ships	Aisles, dining areas, and lounges	Staterooms and compartments
Hotels/Motels/Hospitals/Libraries	Lobbies, stairways, elevators, corridors, public rooms, meeting and banquet rooms, wards	Guest rooms, executive offices, staff lounges, private rooms, and waiting rooms
Professional Offices		Reception areas and consultation rooms of doctors, dentists, lawyers, etc.
Theaters/Bowling Alleys	Lobbies, stairways, lounges, and aisles	

Dependent on size and volume of customers.

Courtesy American Hotel and Motel Association.

Glossary

Reprinted with permission of The Carpet and Rug Institute, from The Carpet Specifier's Handbook, 1974 (Dalton, Georgia: The Carpet and Rug Institute, 1973), pp. 92–106. Copyright 1973 by The Carpet and Rug Institute.

Abraded Yarns. Continuous filament yarns in which filaments have been cut or abraded at intervals and given additional twist to produce a certain degree of hairiness. Abraded yarns are usually plied or twisted with other yarns before using.

Absorption. The ability of a fiber, yarn, or fabric to attract and hold gasses or liquids within its pores.

Acrylics. In the carpet industry, refers to acrylic and modacrylic fibers. Acrylic fiber is a polymer composed of at least 85% by weight of acrylonitrile units. Modacrylic fiber is a polymer composed of less than 85% but at least 35% by weight of acrylonitrile units. Acrylics come only in staple form and are noted for their high durability, stain-resistance, and wool-like appearance.

Affinity. The tendency of two substances to chemically unite as fiber or dyestuff.

American Oriental. A term applied to loom-made American carpets of the Axminster or Wilton weave which have been manufactured in the color and pattern designs of Oriental rugs. Being without sizing, these American-made carpets are soft and pliable and can therefore be folded like an Oriental. The sheen or luster distinguishes this type of American carpet from the other weaves.

Antistatic. Ability of a fabric to disperse electrostatic charges to prevent the build-up of static electricity.

Average Stiffness. Average weight in grams per denier that will stretch fiber 1%.

Axminster. One of the basic weaves used in making carpets. The pile tufts in this weave are mechanically inserted and bound to the back in a manner similar to the hand knotting of Oriental rugs, making possible almost unlimited combinations of colors and patterns. *See* weaving.

BCF. Bulked continuous filament nylon. The highly bulked fibers have a trilobular or triskelion cross section, which gives them greater covering power than round, cross-section fibers possess.

Backing. Material that forms the back of the carpet, regardless of the type of construction. (1) Primary back: In a tufted carpet, the material to which surface yarns are attached. May be made of jute, kraftcord, cotton, woven or nonwoven synthetics. (2) Secondary back: Also called "double backing." Any material (jute, woven or nonwoven synthetics, scrim, foam, or cushion) laminated to the primary back.

Back Seams. While all carpet seams are located on the back or underside of the carpet, those made when the carpet is turned over or face down are called "back seams," while those made with the carpet face up are called "face seams."

Bank. Name applied to a setting machine yarn creel.

Baseboard. A board skirting the lower edge of a wall.

Beam. Large, horizontal cylinders or spools. The warp yarns are wound on beams located back of the line of weave. The woven fabric is wound on a beam located usually in front, just below the line of weave.

Bearding. Long fiber fuzz on loop pile fabrics. Caused by fiber snagging and inadequate anchorage.

Beat-Up. (1) The action of the lay and reed when forcing the filling to the fell of the cloth. (2) The point in the timing cycle of the above operation. (3) The number of tufts per inch of length in a warp row of pile. Used in connection with Axminster, Chenille, and other carpets not woven over wires. Synonymous with "wire" in Wilton, velvet, etc.

Bent Needles. (1) Needles in the tufting machine permanently pushed out of place causing a streak or grinning, running lengthwise because of off standard tuft spacing across the width. (2) A needle in the Jacquard that is out of alignment with punched hole in pattern cards.

Binding. A strip sewed over a carpet edge for protection against unraveling and/or to change its appearance.

Binding Yarn. Cotton or rayon yarn running lengthwise of the woven fabric, used "to bind" the pile tufts firmly; often called "crimp warp" or "binder warp."

Bleeding. Loss of color when wet due to improper dyeing or from the use of poor dyestuffs. Fabrics that bleed will stain fabrics in contact with them when wet.

Blend. A fabric containing a mixture of two or more fibers or yarns, or a combination of two or more fibers spun into a yarn.

Bobbin. A spool-like device made of various materials, shapes, and constructions with a head at one or both ends and a hole through its length or barrel for placement on a spindle or skewer. It is used to hold yarn for spinning, weaving, or sewing.

Body. The compact, solid, firm, or full feel of a fabric.

Bonded Urethane Cushion. A carpet cushion made from trim generated from urethane foam product manufacture which has been granulated and bonded to form a porous foam material and fabricated into foam sheets.

Braided. Reversible oval or round rugs produced from braided strips of new or used material.

Breaking Strength. Ability of a fabric to resist rupture by evenly applied tension.

Expressed as pounds of force applied to 1 inch width in warpwise or fillingwise direction.

Broadloom. An obsolete term originally used to denote carpet produced in widths wider than 6 feet. Was at one time used to identify "high quality." It is no longer an acceptable term in the carpet industry, the preferred word being simply "carpet."

Brocade. A carpet or rug in which a raised pattern or engraved effect is formed using heavy twisted yarn tufts on a ground of straight fibers, the colors of which are often the same.

Brussels. A term formerly, but now rarely, used to describe a loop pile or round-wire carpet woven on the Wilton loom.

Brussels Pitch. 252 or 256 dents per 27 inches in width.

Buckling (Also Puckers). A carpet that does not lay flat on the floor and contains ridges. Can be caused by uneven beam tension, dimensional instability, and putting together mismatched carpet. Failure to stretch wall-to-wall installations sufficiently will also contribute buckles.

Bulking. Processing yarn, usually by mechanical means, to fluff it up and give more coverage with the same weight. Also known as texturizing and lofting.

Bullnose. Colloquial name for Step Return.

Burling. An inspection process following carpet construction to correct loose tufts, etc.; also the process of replacing missing tufts by hand.

Cam Loom. A loom in which the shedding is performed by means of cams. A velvet loom.

Carpet. The general designation for fabric used as a floor covering. It is occasionally used incorrectly in the plural as "carpets" or "carpeting." The preferred usage today is "carpet" in both singular and plural form. It may be used as an adjective, as in "carpeted floors."

Carpet Cushion. A term used to describe any kind of material placed under carpet to provide softness when it is walked on. Not only does carpet cushion provide a softer feel underfoot, it usually provides added acoustical benefits and longer wear life for the carpet. In some cases the carpet cushion is attached to the carpet when it is manufactured. Also referred to as "lining," "padding," or "underlay," although "carpet cushion" is the preferred term.

Catcher Threads. Warp threads in chenille Axminster carpets which attach the chenille fur to the carpet backing structure.

Cellulose. A carbohydrate of complex molecular structure which forms the basic framework of plant cells and walls. Used as a basic raw material in making rayon.

Chain. (1) The binder warp yarn that works over and under the filling shots of the carpet. (2) Axminster loom: refers to the endless chain that carries the tube frames. (3) Dobby loom: refers to the endless chain of pattern selector bars.

Chain Binders. Yarns running warpwise (lengthwise) in the back of a woven carpet, binding construction yarns together in a woven construction.

Chenille. A pile fabric woven by the insertion of a prepared weft row of surface yarn tufts in a "fur" or "caterpillar" form through very fine but strong cotton "catcher" warp yarns, and over a heavy woolen backing yarn.

Cockling. A curliness or crimpiness appearing in the cut face pile as a result of a yarn condition.

Comb. An open-top reed.

Comber Board (Also Comper Board). (1) The part of the Brussels Card Jacquard mechanism that raises all face yarns simultaneously for the insertion of the bottom filling shot. (2) The part of the Fine Index Jacquard through which the lingoes are threaded to hold them in place.

Combination. A term which refers to yarns or fabrics: (1) A combination yarn is composed of two or more yarns having the same or different fibers or twists; e.g., one yarn may have a high twist; the other, little or no twist. (2) A combination fabric is one which uses the above yarns.

Commercial Matching. Matching of colors within acceptable tolerances, or with a color variation that is barely detectable to the naked eye.

Construction. The method by which carpet is made, combining the pile fibers to the backing materials. The term applied to woven, tufted, and knitted carpet.

Continuous Filament. Continuous strand of synthetic fiber extruded in yarn form, without the need for spinning which all natural fibers require.

Cop. A centerless package of filling yarn suitable for insertion into a shuttle.

Cotton. A soft, white, fibrous substance composed of the hairs clothing the seeds of an erect, freely branching tropical plant (cotton plant). (1) Thread spun from cotton. (2) Fabric made of cotton.

Count. (1) A number identifying yarn size or weight per unit of length or vice versa depending on the particular system being used. (2) Count of fabric is indicated by the number of warp ends and filling ends per inch.

Cover. Descriptive of how the face yarn covers the back.

Crab. A hand device usually used for stretching carpet in a small area where a power stretcher or knee kicker cannot be used.

Creel. A frame device which holds cones of yarn, which are fed through tubing into the needles of a tufting machine.

Creeling. The process of mounting yarn packages on the frame.

Crib/Axminster Loom. Refers to the frame work that carries the pattern spool chain.

Crimp. Processing yarn, usually by heat or pressure, to fix a wavy texture and increase bulk.

Crimping. Processing of yarns, usually by heat, steam, or pressure, to introduce and/or set a wavy texture and give increased bulk.

Crocking. Term used to describe excess color rubbing off as the result of improper dye penetration, fixation, or selection.

Cropping. The passage of carpet under a revolving cylinder fitted with cutting blades to obtain a level surface and a uniform height of pile.

Cross-Dyed. Multicolored effects produced in a fabric with fibers of different dye affinities.

Cross-Seams. Seams made by joining the ends of carpet together.

Cushion-Back Carpet. A carpet having a cushioning lining, padding, or underlay material as an integral part of its backing.

Custom-Tufted. Carpets or rugs in which pile yarns are manually tufted with hand machines or by narrow-width tufting machines.

Cut. A length of fabric, such as carpet.

Cut Pile. A fabric, the face of which is composed of cut ends of pile yarn.

Cylinder. The part of the Jacquard that supports and holds the punched pattern cards in position while the plungers or needles that control the yarn selection pass through the card. This "cylinder" is not cylindrical in shape but is frequently 4-, 5-, or 6-sided.

Dead (Pile yarn). The pile yarn in a Wilton carpet (usually figured) which remains hidden in the backing structure when not forming a pile tuft.

Deep-Dyed. Refers to dye penetration in carpet fibers which permits clear, true carpet colors that retain their brillance for the life of the carpet.

Deflected Needle. Needles in the tufting machine that are pushed aside by a warp end in the backing cloth causing a streak or "grinning" running lengthwise because of off-standard tuft spacing across the width.

Delustered Nylon. Nylon whose normally high sheen is reduced by surface treatment.

Denier. Unit of weight for the size of a single filament. The higher the denier, the heavier the yarn. Denier is equivalent to the number of grams per 9,000 meters.

Density. The amount of pile packed into a given volume of carpet, usually measured in ounces of pile yarn per unit volume.

Density Height. The square of the density multiplied by the pile height; a criterion by which the potential wear life of different carpet grades can be compared theoretically. The assumption is made in the use of this criterion that the fibers in the materials being compared are of equal quality, and all other factors are constant. For example, if a carpet has a density of 32 and a pile height of .25 inches, a 25% increase in the pile height would mean a corresponding 25% increase in the durability of the carpet. However, if the density of the carpet were increased by 25%, the durability would have been increased by 66%.

Dent. (1) The space between wires of reed or heddles or harness through which the warp ends are drawn. (2) The space between two chains in a fabric.

Differential Dyeing Fibers (Dye-variant fibers). Fibers, natural or man-made, so treated or modified in composition that their affinity for dyes becomes changed, i.e., to be reserved, dye lighter or dye darker than normal fibers, dependent upon the particular dyes and methods of application employed.

Dimensional Stability. Tendency of a fabric to retain its size and shape; may be brought about by chemical treatment or mechanical means; e.g., a secondary backing adds dimensional stability to carpet.

Dirty Back. Excess face yarn showing on the back of carpet. The usual causes are poor timing, insufficient tension on the face yarn, excessively bulky face yarns, and insufficient stuffers.

Dobby. A device that selects the rotation in which one or more of a group of harnesses are raised over a filling shot. Can float an end over as many filling shots as desired. Produces geometric patterns.

Domestic. Describes carpet made by skilled craftsmen in the United States.

Dope Dyed (Same as Spun Dyed and Solution Dyed). This applies to synthetic fibers only. The coloring materials are added to the solution before extruding through a spinneret to form the filament.

Double Back. A woven or nonwoven material adhered to the backing of some carpet as additional reinforcement, to provide greater dimensional stability and improved tuft bind. Also known as scrim back.

Double Beating. Two successive beats of the reed to press heavy or bulky filling in place.

Draw. The manner and rotation in which the warp ends are placed in the loom heddles and reeds.

Drawing-In or Drawing-Up. The process of placing the warp ends through the heddles and reeds of the loom.

Draw-Straight. The ends are drawn in straight or direct sequence from first to last harness in the plan.

Drop Match. When the design in a carpet must be dropped in the next combining width of carpet to maintain the pattern.

Drugget. A course, heavy imported fabric, felted or plain woven, usually of all wool. The designs are either woven into a fabric or printed.

Drying Cans (Cylinders). Heated rotating cylinders over which textile materials are passed to dry them.

Dutchman. Colloquial name for a narrow strip of carpet side seamed to standard width broadloom to compensate for unusual offsets, sloping walls, etc., but never used as a substitute for good planning and proper stretching techniques.

Dye Beck. A large vat into which roll lengths are submerged for piece dyeing.

Dyeing. The process of coloring materials; impregnating fabric with dyestuff.
  1. Solution dyed: Synthetic yarn which is spun from a colored solution; the filament is thus impregnated with the pigment.

2. Stock dyed: Fibers are dyed before spinning.

3. Yarn (or skein) dyed: Yarn dyed before being fabricated into carpet.

4. Piece dyeing unfinished carpet: Carpet dyed "in a piece" after tufting or weaving but before other finishing processes such as latexing or foaming.

5. Cross dyeing: Method of dyeing fabrics with dyestuffs which have different affinities for different types of yarns.

6. Space dyeing: Process whereby different colors are "printed" along the length of yarn before it is manufactured into carpet.

7. Continuous dyeing: The process of dyeing carpet in a continuous production line, rather than piece-dyeing separate lots. Most often done on Kusters continuous dyeing equipment which flows on dyestuffs, as distinguished from submerging carpet in separate dye becks.

Dyestuff. The substance which adds color to textiles by absorption into the fiber.

Elasticity. The ratio of stress to strain within the elastic limit of the material.

Electostatic Flocking. The process used for the majority of flocked commercial carpets. Specially treated fibers are charged by an electrostatic field. When the charged fibers encounter the object to be coated, they are moving vertically at a high speed and they become firmly embedded in the adhesive.

Embossed. In carpet, the type of pattern formed when heavy twisted tufts are used in a ground of straight yarns to create an engraved appearance. Both the straight and twisted yarns are often of the same color.

End. (1) An individual warp yarn. A warp is composed of a number of ends. (2) A short length or remnant.

Extended Length. The length of the face pile yarn used to make 1 inch of tufted carpet.

Face Seams. Seams, either sewed or oo

mented, that are made without turning the entire carpet over or face down. They are made during installation where it is not possible to make back seams.

Fadeometer. Standard laboratory device for testing a fabric's resistance to sunlight.

Fastness. Property of dye to retain its color when cloth is exposed to sun, perspiration, atmosphhere, washing, or other color-destroying agents. The term fastness is a relative one. A dye may be reasonably fast to washing and only moderately fast to light. Fastness of color is tested by standard procedures.

Fell or Fell of the Cloth. The line to which a filling end is beaten by the reed.

Felt or Felted. An inexpensive rug, usually woven in plain colors (or stenciled or printed), in plain flat weaves and felted.

Felting. The process of pressing or matting together various types of hair or fibers to form a continuous fabric, known as felt.

Fiber. Any substance, natural or synthetic, strong enough to be used in thread or yarn form for processing as a textile.

Fiber Cushion. A term used to describe carpet cushion made by the needlepunch process out of animal hair or jute material, or a blend. Some constructions are made with a rubber face and backed by hair or fiber.

Fiber Rugs. Rugs made of specially prepared paper yarns in combination with cotton and wool yarns. Fiber rugs are reversible, come in plain or twill weaves, and are often sized.

Filament. A single strand of any kind of fiber, natural or synthetic. In textile use, filaments of natural fiber must be spun into yarns, and synthetic filaments are extruded as yarns.

Filler. Fuller's earth or clay—or similar material—used in the mix of latex and attached cushion.

Filling Yarn. Yarns, usually of cotton, jute, or kraftcord, running across a woven fabric and used with the chain yarns to bind the pile tufts to the backing yarns.

Film Yarn (Cut-film or slit-film yarns). Yarn composed of one or more continuous narrow strips of man-made film (usually slit-film, but strips may be extruded), or incorporating one or more strips as a major component.

Finishing. A final process through which fabrics are put in order to prepare them for the market; such as bleaching, scouring, calendering, embossing, rapping, mercerizing, water-proofing, or moth-proofing.

Flexibility. The property of bending without breaking.

Float. (1) A planned part of the design in which the face yarn is carried over two or more wires. (2) A defect in the face of carpet resulting from a long loose end of face yarn that is not securely fastened into the back.

Flocking. Short, chopped fiber or flock is adhered, usually by electrostatic processes, to a base fabric, resulting in a short-pile material with a velvety texture.

Floor Mat. Carpet usually less than 22½ inches wide and less than 7½ square feet in area.

Fluffing. Appearance on carpet surface of loose fiber fragments left during manufacture; not a defect but a characteristic which disappears after carpet use and vacuuming.

Foam Rotary Shampooing. A shampooing method which reduces drying time to 30 to 60 minutes. The new equipment consists of a foamer attachment (a self-contained solution tank and foam builder) which fits on any rotary machine. One man does the shampooing and another removes the heavy dirty suds with a wet vacuum.

Frames. Racks at back of the Wilton loom holding spools from which yarns are fed into the loom, each frame holding separate colors; thus a 3-frame Wilton has three colors in the design.

Free Form. A floor area bounded by walls and of nonrectangular shape. Sometimes called "form-fit area."

Frieze. (Pronounced "free-zay") A tightly

twisted yarn that gives a rough, nubby appearance to carpet pile.

Frieze Yarn. A hard-twisted yarn used commonly in plain fabrics to effect a rough, knotty, textured appearance in the surface pile.

Full Roll. An unbound cut of carpet, described in the carpet industry as being over 30 feet in length, by the width of the production run from which it was cut.

Fuzzing. Hairy effect on fabric surface caused by wild fibers or slack yarn twist, by fibers slipping out of yarn or contour in either service or wet cleaning. It is corrected by shearing in manufacturing and by the professional cleaner. Carpet of continuous filament yarn is fuzzed by filament snagging and breaking.

Gage Or Gauge. The distance between two needle points expressed in fraction of an inch. Applies to both knitting and tufting.

Gauge/Pitch. The number of ends of surface yarn counting across the width of carpet. In woven carpet, pitch is the number of ends of yarn in 27 inches of width; e.g., 216 divided by 27 = 8 ends per inch. In tufted carpet, gauge also means the number of ends of surface yarn per inch counting across the carpet; e.g., ⅛ gauge = 8 ends per inch. To convert gauge to pitch, multiply ends per inch by 27; e.g., 1/10 gauge is equivalent to 270 pitch, or 10 ends per inch x 27. One-eighth gauge is 8 ends of yarn per inch x 27 = 216 pitch.

Gauge Wire. A type of standing wire used with an extra filling yarn to control the height of the pile.

Grass. Rugs made of certain long jointless grasses, twisted with cotton threads into yarns. Grass rugs are usually reversible and come in plain weave and color.

Grate or Grid or Hook Plate. The part of the Fine Index Jacquard in which the bottom hooks of Jacquard hook wires are set when the top hook is not engaged by the griff. It is also used to raise all the remaining face yarns that were not selected to be raised by the griff to permit the insertion of the bottom shot.

Greige Goods. (Pronounced "gray goods") Term designating carpet just off the tufting machine and in an undyed or unfinished state.

Griff or Griffe. (1) The part of the Fine Index Jacquard consisting of members containing the metal knives. (2) Also applied to the metal lifting knives used to lift the hook selected to be up at the correct time.

Grin. A term used to indicate the condition where the backing of the carpet shows between the rows of pile tuft; e.g., some carpet may show the backing when layed over the nosing of a step.

Ground Color. The background color against which the top colors create the pattern or figure in the design.

Hair. Animal fiber other than wool or silk.

Hand. The "feel" of a carpet in the hand—determined by such factors as pile height, quality and kind of fibers, type of construction, type of backing, and dimensional stability.

Harness. (1) The frame holding the heddles through which the warp ends are drawn and then raised and lowered to form the shed. (2) The cords that connect the Jacquard hooks to the lingo heddles.

Heather. A multicolor effect provided by intimately blending fibers of different colors prior to spinning carpet yarn.

Heat Set. Stabilization of yarns to insure no change in size or shape; the process of heat setting in an autoclave, using superheated steam under pressure.

Heddle. A series of vertical cords or wires, each of which has in the middle a loop or eye which receives a warp yarn. The two heddle frames, each carrying a set of chain warp yarns, rise and fall alternately forming the shed through which the weft shuttle passes.

Heddle frame. The frame on which the heddles are mounted.

Hessian. Plain cloth, usually of jute, containing single yarns of approximately the same count in warp and weft.

High Density. A term to describe a material with heavier than normal weight-per-unit volume.

High Density Foam. Rubber product applied as a liquid foam, then cured, to form an integral part of the carpet back. The minimum standards are weight: 38 ounces per square yard, thickness: ⅛ inch, density: 25 pounds per cubic foot.

High Low. A multilevel pile, sometimes combining cut and looped surface yarns.

Hooked Rugs. Yarn or strips of cloth inserted into a prewoven cloth stenciled with a pattern. Usually a hand or single needle process. Modern tufting is mechanized hooking.

Hooks (Also Wire Hooks). (1) The vertical wires in a Jacquard that are hooked on each end and the bottom hook attached by cords to the lingo heddles carrying the pattern yarn. The top hooks are positioned by the needles to either be caught onto or clear the lifting knife in the griff. In most Jacquards, the hooks that are picked up by the lifting knives raise a face yarn end over the filling shot and/or wire. (2) The hook-shaped stamped metal latches used to catch the pile wire after it is beaten up and retard the wire's tendency to jump or fall toward the reed.

Hopper. The assembly that engages the pile wire head, drawing it from front of wire set and returning it under pile shed.

Hot Melt. A blend of polymer and filling applied in a heated state to a carpet back, to lock in surface yarns and for lamination.

Indoor/Outdoor. (Obsolete term, see outdoor carpet.) The first carpet produced for outdoor use was named indoor/outdoor carpet. Over a period of time this term was erroneously thought by retailers and consumers to indicate "that if it is okay for outdoor use it has superior qualities indoors." Since this statement is generally incorrect, the carpet industry wants to avoid perpetuating this term.

Ingrain Carpet. A double-faced pile-less carpet using colored filling yarns to make the design. The fabric is reversible and the designs and colors on the face and back will also be in reverse positions. This type was also called Scotch or Kidderminster.

Ingraining. Mixing and weaving threads of various colors.

Jacquard. The pattern control on a Wilton loom. A chain of perforated cardboard "cards" punched according to the design elements, which when brought into position activates this mechanism by causing it to select the desired color of yarn to form the design on the pile surface. The unselected colors are woven "dormant" through the body of the fabric.

Jacquard Cards. Punched cards (usually laced together) which are presented to the Jacquard in sequence, for the selection of lifting of the pile ends as required for patterning.

Jaspe. Irregular stripes of two hues, shades, or values of the same color used to produce a particular effect on the pile yarn of plain or even designed fabrics. Various jaspe effects can be produced by varying the twist of the yarn.

Jerker Bar (Tufting). The guide or thread jerker which takes up slack tufting yarn during the upstroke of the needle and controls the amount supplied for the backstroke.

Jute. A fibrous skin between the bark and stalk of a plant native to India and the Far East. Shredded and spun, it forms a strong and durable yarn used in carpet backing to add strength, weight, and stiffness.

Kemp. Coarse, brittle white fiber occurring frequently in "nonblooded" carpet wools. These fibers do not accept dye and consequently an excess could be prominent and undesirable.

Kidderminster Carpet. Originated in a town of that name in England. Similar to Ingrain Carpet.

Kilmarnock Carpet. Similar to Ingrain Carpet.

Knee Kicker. A short tool with gripping "teeth" at one end and a padded cushion at the other, used in making small stretches during carpet installation.

Knife. Refer to either of the two steel blades of an Axminster loom that operates as a shear to cut and make the pile ends.

Knitting. A method of fabricating a carpet in one operation, as in weaving. Surface and backing yarns are looped together with a stitching yarn on machines with three sets of needles.

Kraftcord. A tightly twisted yarn made from plant fiber, used as a backing yarn in carpet weaves.

Kusters Dyeing. Named after the Kusters dye machine. This is a piece dyeing technique that allows uniform and continuous dyeing in great quantities. A new and major technique for the dyeing of tufted carpet.

Laminated. Fabric composed of layers of cloth joined together.

Lash Board or Lifting Board. The part of the Brussels Jacquard that contains keyhole shaped notches in a board through which lash cords with positioned knots are threaded and then to lift the face yarn selected by the pattern card for the insertion of the wire and shot.

Latex. A milky, rubbery fluid found in several seed plants, and used to seal the back of carpet and for lamination. May be used on tufted or woven carpet.

Latexing. A term used to describe the application of a natural or synthetic latex compound to the back of carpet.

Lay. (1) A collective name given to the parts of the loom that perform the operation of beating up. The parts include reed, reed cap, race plate, shuttles, shuttle brakes, picker sticks, lug, cams. (2) The tendency of pile tufts or loops to lean in a certain direction.

Leno Weave. Weave in which warp yarns, arranged in pairs, are twisted around one another between "picks" of weft yarn.

Levelling Board or Padder. The part of the Brussels Jacquard that assists in properly positioning the needles or plungers that were pushed back by the unpunched portions of the pattern card.

Level Loop. A construction in which the carpet face yarns are tufted or woven into loops of the same pile height.

Lingo or Lingoe. The weight attached by a cord to the heddles to assist in holding a taut vertical position.

Lining. *See* Carpet Cushion.

Lip. The chain and/or stuffer left on the edge of carpet after it has been cut.

Loom. A machine in which yarn or thread is woven into a fabric by the crossing of the warp or chain by other threads, called the weft or filling, at right angles to the warp threads.

Looped Pile. Pile surface in which looped yarns are left uncut. In woven carpets, sometimes referred to as "round wire."

Loopers. The thin, flat steel components that move beside the inserted needles and hook the tufting yarn into loops.

Low Rows. Rows of excessively low pile height across the width of the carpet. Usually due to run out of the final bits of face yarn on the spools on the Axminster loom.

Luster. Sheen of yarns, fiber, or finished fabrics.

Luster Fabric. Any cut pile fabric woven with surface yarns spun from special types of staple and chemically washed, like hand-woven Oriental fabrics, to give a bright sheen or luster.

Lustering. Finishing process produces luster on yarns, cloth.

Marker. (1) A distinguishing threadline woven in the back toward the right-hand edge to enable the workroom or installer to assemble breadths of carpet and have the pile lay in one and same direction. (2) A pattern marking point of a distinguishing color woven into the back close to each edge to enable the workroom or the installer to assemble breadths of carpet and match the pattern when working on the under side.

Match Set, or Drop. In a set-match carpet pattern, the figure matches straight across on each side of the carpet width; in a drop-match, the figure matches midway of the design; in a quarter drop-match, the figure matches one-quarter of the length of the repeat on the opposite side.

Mending (Picking). A hand operation carried out on carpet before finishing to remove any knots and loose ends of yarn, to insert pile tufts where missing and to replace and repair backing yarns as required.

Metallic Fiber. A manufactured fiber composed of metal, plastic-coated metal, metal-coated plastic, or a core completely covered by metal. The most important characteristic of metallic fiber in carpet is to reduce build-up of static electricity.

Mill End. The remainder of a roll carpet, generally described in the carpet industry as being over 9 feet in length, but under 21 feet in length, by the width of the roll from which it was cut.

Mil. A unit commonly used for measuring the diameter of textile monofilaments— 1/1,000 inch.

Mitre. The junction of two pieces of carpet, wood, or other material at an angle; usually 45° to form a right angle, but may be any combination of angles.

Modacrylics. Refer to Acrylics.

Molded Rubber Back. A new kind of carpet backing. Liquid rubber is coated on the carpet back and then rolled out with an embossed roller.

Molding. A strip, generally of wood, at the bottom of a baseboard or wall, to cover the joint between wall and floor.

Monofilament. A filament large and strong enough to be used directly as a yarn for making textiles through any established process.

Moresque. Single strands of different colors of yarn twisted or plied together to form one multicolored yarn.

Multifilament. Yarns made of many filaments plied or spun together. The finer the filaments spun together, the softer and more luxurious the yarn and textiles made from it.

Nap. The pile on the surface of a carpet or rug.

Narrow Carpet. Fabric woven 27 inches and 36 inches in width.

Natural Gray Yarn. Unbleached and un-dyed yarn spun from a blend of black, brown, or gray wools.

Needle. (1) Jacquard loom: The horizontal wires, rods, or plungers. The forward and backward movement of which is controlled by the pattern punch cards. One end is placed into a needle board and the ends extend slightly beyond the board surface. The other end projects into a levelling board, padder, needle box, or spring box. The forward and backward movements position the lash cord knots to be picked up by the lash board, lifting board, or comber board, or the hooks to be picked up by the griff remain in the grate. (2) Axminster loom: Refers to metal rod used to insert a shot of filling yarn. (3) Knitting: The hooks that make the loops. (4) Tufting: The needle with an eye to punch the pile yarn through the backing material. (5) Needlepunching: The needle that stitches the fibers to a base fabric.

Needle Bar. The part of the knitting and tufting machine used to hold the needles in position.

Needle Board. (1) The part of the Jacquard that holds the end of the needles that are presented to the punched cards carried on the cylinder. (2) The base that holds the needles for needlepunching.

Needle Box (Spring Box, Levelling Board, Padder). The part of the Jacquard that holds the opposite ends of the needles to the needle board. Contains springs to reposition the needles pushed back by the unpunched parts of the pattern cards.

Needlepunching. Layers or batts of loose fiber are needled into a core, or scrim, fabric to form a felted or flat-textured material.

A needlepunched fabric can be embossed, printed, or laminated to a cushion, or otherwise finished.

Noil. A by-product in worsted yarn manufacture, consisting of short wool fibers, less than a determined length, which are combed out.

Nonwoven. A fabric made up of a web of fibers held together by a chemical or fibrous bonding agent.

Nosing. The front dividing line of a step, where the top of a riser joins the front of a tread.

Nylon. A synthetic material, of synthetic polyamides derivable from coal, air, and water, which is adapted for fashioning into filaments of extreme toughness, strength, and elasticity.

Odor. Abnormal or obnoxious smells. Usually caused by fungi attacking jute or sulfur compounds in latex back-size.

Oily Wires. A gray or black discoloration across the width of the carpet due to both dirty and oily wire. If oil is colorless, appearance of defect is delayed until carpet is in service and the difference in soiling rate makes it apparent.

Oily Yarn. Soiled yarn running in the warp direction. Not always apparent at time of inspection but is revealed in service by difference in soiling rate. Generally caused by excessive oiling of rings or spinning or twisting equipment.

Olefins. Any long chain synthetic polymer composed of at least 85% by weight of ethylene, propylene, or other olefin units.

Oriental Rugs. Hand-woven rugs made in the Middle East and the Orient.

Outoor Carpet. A term used to describe carpet that has been specially engineered so that all elements of the product will resist the ravages of the sun, rain, and snow. Outdoor carpet is generally made of all synthetic material. Special attention has been paid to sun fade degradation of the pile fiber.

Package-Dyed. Spun and wound yarn, placed on large perforated forms, is colored by dye forced through the perforations.

Padding. *See* Carpet Cushion.

Patent-back Carpet. Carpet so constructed that the fabric can be cut in any direction, without raveling of edges. The edges are joined by tape and adhesives instead of being sewed.

Pattern. (1) Any ornamental feature that is decorative in a fabric and serves to distinguish it from plainness. (2) The sketch to scale showing a design.

Pattern Bars. A series of bars on the tufting machine that are linked together by an endless chain to make a complete pattern. A bar extends across the width of the machine and contains grooves to accommodate each single end of face yarn. The grooves are cut to various predetermined depths to control the pile height by regulating the yarnfeed and obtain a surface pattern.

Pattern Rollers. A combination of rollers on the tufting machine that determines both the pile height and the pattern by controlling speed of the yarnfeed.

Pattern Streaks. Occurs in all patterned carpets to some degree. Sometimes the figures line up in such a way as to be too obvious and objectionable.

Pick. The number of weft yarns shuttled across the warp yarns, and indicating closeness of weave lengthwise. A high-grade Wilton fabric may have 39 picks per inch, or 3 shots of weft to each wire.

Picking. (1) The operation of taking the weft (filling) through the warp shed during weaving. (2) *See* mending.

Picks per Inch. The number of filling insertions required to make 1 inch of fabric.

Piece-Dyed. Entire carpet immersed in dye bath. Used for dyeing tufted carpet.

Pigment. A finely divided, insoluble substance used to deluster or color yarns or fabrics.

Pigmented Yarns. A dull or colored yarn spun from a solution to which a pigment has been added.

Pile. The upright ends of yarn, whether cut or looped, that form the wearing surface of carpet or rugs.

Pile Crush. Bending of pile by constant walking or the pressure of furniture.

Pile Density. The number of tufts both across and lengthwise the carpet. In tufted carpet the measure across the carpet is called needles per inch or gauge. Lengthwise is called stitches per inch.

Pile Height. The height of pile measured from the surface of the back to the top of the pile.

Pile Setting. Brushing done after shampooing to restore the damp pile to its original height. A pile lifting machine or a pile brush is used.

Pile Wire. A metal strip or rod over which the yarn is woven to produce a pile.

Pile Yarn. The yarn used to form the loops or tufts of carpet.

Pilling. A condition in certain fibers in which strands of the fiber separate and become knotted with other strands, causing a rough, spotty appearance. Pilled tufts should never be pulled from carpet, but may be cut off with a sharp scissors at the pile surface.

Pitch. *See* Gauge.

Plain or Flat Weave. A fabric with a flat surface, in plain, twill, or fancy weaves, having a printed, stenciled, or "woven in" design, and generally reversible.

Planting. A method of placing spools of different colors of surface yarn in frames back of Jacquard Wilton looms so that more colors will appear in the design than are supplied in the full solid colors used. These extra "planted" colors are usually arranged in groups of each shade to give added interest to the pattern.

Plied Yarns. Two or more strands, ends, or plys either twisted or otherwise cohesively entwined, intermingled, or entangled into a heavier yarn.

Plush Finish. A term used to describe a dense cut pile carpet in which the surface has a solid "mirrorlike" appearance. The ends of each tuft tend to merge into a common surface.

Ply. The number of strands of yarn twisted together to form a single yarn, as in "2-ply" or "3-ply."

Polyester. A manufactured fiber in which the fiber-forming substance is any long-chain synthetic polymer composed of at least 85% by weight of an ester of a dihydric alcohol and terephthalic acid (p-$HOOC-C_6H_4-COOH$).

Polymer. In synthetics, the basic chemical unit from which fibers are made. It is made of large complex molecules formed by uniting molecules (monomers).

Polypropylene. High-molecular weight paraffin fiber made by the polymerization of propylene (FTC classification Olefin).

Power Stretcher. An extension-type version of the knee kicker, with more "teeth" arranged in a head which can be adjusted for depth of "bite," or used to stretch larger areas of carpet than cannot be handled by the knee kicker.

Primary Backing. The material on which the carpet is constructed. The material to which the visible secondary backing is anchored. Usually jute or polypropylene.

Prime Urethane Cushion. A carpet cushion made from virgin polyether urethane foam slab stacks.

Print-Dyed. The pattern is screen printed on the woven carpet by means of premetalized dyes.

Printed Carpet. Carpet with surface patterns applied by means of dyes used on engraved rollers, wood blocks, or screens.

Printing. The process of producing a pattern with dyestuffs on carpet and rugs. May be done by several methods, such as screen printing (e.g., on Zimmer equipment, which may be flat bed or rotary screen printing), or on roller equipment operating on the relief-printing principle (e.g., Stalwart equipment).

Puckering. A condition in a carpet seam, due to poor layout or unequal stretching, etc., wherein the carpet on one side of the seam is longer or shorter than that on the other side, causing the long side to wrinkle or develop a "pleated" effect.

Quarter. A quarter of a yard, or 9 inches, formerly used as a unit of woven carpet-width measure. A 27-inch carpet was therefore designated ¾ carpet and a 36-inch carpet was known as 4/4 carpet. Today actual feet and inches are given in describing carpet width.

Quarter Drop Match. *See* Match.

Quarter-Round. A length of wood used for finishing moldings and joints between walls and floors, four of which, if placed together along their straight edges, would make a completely circular (i.e., cylindrical) "pole."

Rag Rug. (1) A plain weave made of rag strips, filling, and cotton chain warp. (2) Braided rag strips stitched together by hand or machine.

Random-Sheared. Textured pattern created by shearing some of the top or higher loops and leaving others looped.

Reed. A frame holding thin strips of steel with narrow spaces between them through which the warp ends are drawn in a definite order. The reed is mounted in the lay and used to distribute and spread warp yarns and beat the filling up to the fell of the cloth.

Reed Mark. Streak running in the warp direction caused by loose or bent reed.

Reel Foam Cleaning. Is done with a type of carpet shampooing machine that releases foam and brushes in a cylinder reel action, the same as a pile lifter. In this kind of cleaning, the carpet is first shampooed and then the foam is removed.

Remnant. The remainder of a roll of carpet, generally described in the carpet industry as being under 9 feet in length by the width of the roll from which it was cut.

Repeat. The distance from a point in a pattern figure to the same point where it occurs again, measuring lengthwise of the fabric.

Residual Shrinkage. Amount of shrinkage remaining in a fabric after the decrease in dimensions has been determined by preshrinking; decrease in dimensions of a fabric after washing or dry cleaning.

Resilience. The ability of a carpet fabric or padding to spring back to its original shape or thickness after being crushed or walked upon.

Resist-Printing. A dye-resist agent is printed on tufted carpet prior to piece dyeing.

Restretch. A term applied to the remedial steps necessary for the correction of improperly laid carpet resulting from application of wrong stretching techniques, carpet defects, or undetermined causes.

Reverse Coloring. The process whereby the dominant background colors and the top colors of a fabric are reversed. It can be done in Wilton weaves by changing the yarn colors of each frame.

Round Wire or Looped Pile. A Wilton or velvet carpet woven with the pile yarn uncut.

Roving. A loose cluster of fibers drawn or rubbed into a single strand with very little twist; an intermediate stage between sliver and yarn.

Rows or Wires. The number of lengthwise yarn tufts in 1 inch of carpet. In Axminster or chenille, they are called "rows." In Wilton and velvet, they are known as "wires."

Rubber. A cushioned carpet back which may be applied in various forms, such as contoured, compressed, or slab. Also, a separate rug or carpet cushion.

Rug. A term used to designate soft floor coverings laid on the floor but not fastened to it. As a rule, a rug does not cover the entire floor.

Saponification. Reaction which causes acetate to be converted to regenerated cellulose.

Saxony Finish. A term used to describe a dense cut pile carpet, usually made of heavy yarns that have been plied and heat set, so that each tuft end has a distinguishable appearance.

Scale Drawing. A drawing in which the measurements represented are drawn to a predetermined scale, such as ¼ inch equals 1 foot, so that all elements and dimensions in the drawing are proportional in length and width to the actual room, floor, or building depicted.

Scallops. The up-and-down uneven effect along the edge of carpet caused by indentations where tacks are driven.

Scrambler Box. A device incorporated in some types of tufting pattern attachments, to equalize the distance of travel of all pile ends in the pattern groups repeating across the machine width, and thus avoid problems arising due to differences in tensioning.

Scribing. Transferring the exact irregularities of a wall or other surface onto a piece of carpet, wood, or paper, which is then cut to fit those irregularities.

Scrim Back. A double back made of light, coarse fabric, cemented to a jute or kraftcord or synthetic back in tufted construction. *See* Double Back.

Sculptured. In carpet, this refers to a type of pattern formed when certain tufts are eliminated or pile yarns are drawn tightly to the back to form a specific design in the face of the carpet. The pattern resulting simulates the effect of hand carving.

Seams. *See* Back Seams; Face Seams; Cross-Seams; Side Seams.

Seamless. Without seams.

Secondary Backing. The extra layer of material laminated to the underside of the carpet for additional dimensional stability and body. Usually latex foam, jute, polypropylene, or vinyl.

Seconds. Carpets or rugs rejected for having certain imperfections, flaws, or deviations of weave and marked as "seconds" or "imperfect" by the manufacturer.

Self-Tone. A pattern of two or more shades of the same color. When two shades are used in a pattern or design, it is called "two-tone."

Selvage. The edge of a carpet so finished that it will not ravel or require binding or hemming.

Serging. Also known as "oversewing," this is a method of finishing the edge of carpet. It is customary to serge the side and bind the end.

Serrated or Undulating or Wavy Wires. A wire cut high and low to a plan and combined in a group to rotate in sequence to create a desired pattern in the surface of the carpet.

Set or Drop Match. In a set-match carpet pattern, the figure matches straight across on each side of the narrow carpet width; in a drop-match, the figure matches midway of the design; in a quarter dropmatch, the figure matches one-quarter of the length of the repeat on the opposite side.

Setting. The process of preparing a pattern for the Axminster loom by winding the specified yarn the color on a spool in the sequence required for weaving.

Sewing Pole. Any piece of wood or other material, more or less rounded, over which carpet may be laid in order to facilitate sewing and other related operations. Most installers prefer a wooden pole about 4 inches in diameter that has been slightly flattened on one side.

Shading. An apparent change of color in carpet pile caused as light is reflected in different ways when pile fibers are bent; not a defect, but a characteristic especially of cut pile fabrics, including upholstery and clothing.

Shag. A low-density type of carpet of cut and/or loop pile construction wherein the pile surface texture has a random tumbled appearance. This effect is created in use by the random layover of the pile yarn in all directions, as distinguished from the normal upright position of the pile in plush carpet.

Shearing. The process in manufacture in which the fabric is drawn under revolving cutting blades as in a lawn mower, in order to produce a smooth face on the fabric.

Shed. The "V"-shaped opening behind the race plate that is formed by warp ends as they are raised and lowered by their respective harnesses for the insertion of the filling.

Sheen-Type. A rug having a high luster, usually produced by chemical washing.

Shooting or Sprouting. Individual strands of yarn protruding about the surface of the pile. These may be extra long ends of tufts which were not sheared at the mill, pieces of backing material which have risen above the surface, loose ends which were not secured firmly, or occasionally the untwisting of the tightly twisted tufts in a twist weave carpet. This condtion of sprouting or shooting does not mean that the fabric is coming apart, for it does no damage. It is only necessary to clip or shear these loose ends even with pile surface. The sprouting yarns should not be pulled out.

Short Roll. An unbound cut of carpet, generally described in the carpet industry as being over 21 feet in length, but under 30 feet, by the width of the roll from which it was cut.

Shot. The number of weft yarns in relation to each row of pile tufts crosswise in the loom. A 2-shot fabric is one having two weft yarns for each row of pile tufts; a 3-shot fabric has three weft yarns for each row of tufts.

Shrinkage. The contraction of fabrics after wetting and redrying.

Shuttle. In weaving, a boat-shaped, wooden instrument which holds the bobbin from which the weft yarns unwind as the shuttle passes through the warp shed.

Shuttle Box. The receivers on each side of the loom that catch the shuttle as it comes through the shed of the loom.

Side Seams. Seams running the length of the carpet, adding to the width. Also called length seams.

Sizing. Operation consisting of applying starch, gelatin, oil, wax, or any other ingredient onto yarn to aid the process of fabrication or to control fabric characteristics. Warp sizing is usually referred to as slashing.

Skein Dyed Yarn. Surface yarn spun from white staple and dyed in kettles or vats by immersion in skein form.

Sliver. A loose, soft, untwisted strand or rope of fibers.

Smash. Breakage of a large number of warp ends because of some irregularity in the loom function.

Smyrna. A reversible, double-plied run, woven from chenille fur strips without the backing characteristic of the chenille weave. The binding yarns are wool, cotton, jute, or paper.

Soil Retardant. Agent applied to carpet pile yarns to resist soiling.

Solution Dyed. Dye or colored pigments added to solution before extrusion of synthetic filaments.

Space-Dyed. A special machine applies two or more colors to the yarn at predetermined intervals prior to tufting.

Specific Gravity. Ratio of the weight of a given volume of the fiber to an equal volume of water taken as standard at stated temperatures.

Spike Roll. A spiked cylinder at the front of the loom that controls the number of rows per inch in the carpet by regulating the speed with which it advances the cloth.

Spinning. (1) Chemical Spinning: The process of producing man-made fibers, including the extrusion of the spinning liquid through a spinneret into a coagulating medium and the winding of the filaments onto bobbins or in cake form. (2) Mechanical Spinning: Twisting together and drawing out short fibers into continuous strands of yarn.

Splush Finish. A term used to describe a semidense cut pile carpet, about halfway in appearance between a shag and a plush. The tufts lay less irregularly than shag, but not as regular as a plush.

Sponge Cushion. A carpet cushion made of chemically blown sponge, including both waffle or flat surfaces.

Spool. (1) A cylinder with end flanges on which yarn is wound. (2) Axminster: a flanged interlocking ended cylinder used in "setting" on which pile yarn is wound in a predetermined sequence to make a pattern.

Sprouting. Protrusion of individual tuft or yarn ends above the surface pile level of carpet but may be clipped off with a scissors level with the pile surface.

Spun-Dyed (Mass Pigmented, Dope Dyed). Descriptive of colored man-made fibers in which the coloring matter is incorporated in the substrate before extrusion as filament.

Stabilizing. Treating a fabric so that it will not shrink or stretch more than a certain percentage.

Standing Wire. A term applied to pile forming wires that are fixed and extend through the reed. The height of the wire controls the height of the pile ends.

Staple. Fiber in the natural, unprocessed state, usually in short lengths, which must be spun or twisted into yarn, as opposed to continuous filament.

Staple Fiber. The short lengths into which filament yarns are cut to enable them to be spun on conventional spinning machinery.

Staple Nylon. Nylon composed of specially engineered fibers cut into short staple for spinning yarns.

Static Shock. The discomfort experienced by a person touching a conductive object and grounding to earth a static charge accumulated in the body by friction.

Stay Tacking. Temporary tacking of the carpet to hold the stretch.

Stiffness. Ability of a fiber or fabric to resist bending.

Stitch. The number of lengthwise yarn tufts in 1 inch of tufted carpet.

Stitch Length. The length of yarn from which a stitch is made.

Stock-Dyed Yarn. Surface yarn spun from fibers that have already been dyed in staple form in large quantities. Compare Skein-dyed yarn.

Stop Marks. A mark across the width of tufted carpet caused by off-standard feed relationship of either yarn or cloth feed or both on the start up on the machine.

Streak. A discoloration extended as an irregular stripe in the carpet.

Stretch. The lengthening of a filament, yarn, or fabric when stress is applied.

Stria or Striped. A striped effect obtained by twisting loosely two strands of one shade of yarn with one strand of a lighter or darker shade. The single yarn appears like irregular stripes.

Stuffers. Extra yarns running lengthwise through a woven fabric to increase weight and strength.

Swatch. Small piece of fabric used as a representative sample of the goods.

Tabby Weave. A type of weaving used to give a staggered diagonal pattern across the weft yarns. Most commonly used in loomed carpet construction.

Tablet Test. Standard testing method for carpet flammability using an ignition tablet (or methenamine "pill") under controlled conditions.

TAK Dyeing. Another new process in which dye is applied over a continuous dyed fabric by a controlled "sprinkle" technique. This allows more color and pattern interest in tufted carpet.

Take Up (Also Crimp). The difference in distance between two points of a yarn as it lies in the fabric and the same two points when the yarn has been removed and straightened, expressed as a percent of the extended length. Similar to extended length used in tufting except that extended length is linear and the base is 1 inch of carpet.

Take Up Roll. Refers to the shaft that winds up the cloth after it leaves the "spike roll."

Tapestry. A term formerly, but now rarely, used to describe a looped pile fabric woven on the velvet loom.

Template. A pattern, generally of paper or cardboard, for shaping carpet to be cut.

Tenacity. Stress applied to produce a particular elongation in a fiber. The breaking tenacity is the stress required to elongate a fiber to the breaking point.

Tensile Strength. Breaking strain of yarns or fabrics. High tensile strength means strong yarns or fabrics.

Texture. A surface effect obtained by using different heights of pile or two or more forms of yarn, or by alternating the round and cut pile wires, by "brocade" engraving, simulated or actual carving or shaving with an electric razor, or other special treatment of the design, to give added interest beyond that provided by the woven design or tones.

Thermal Conductivity. The measurement of heat flow through a material.

Thick and Thin Yarns. Specialty yarns of varying thickness.

Threading. (1). The process of drawing the yarn ends through the tube frame which prepares pile spools for the Axminster loom. (2) Same as "drawing in."

Three-Quarter Carpet. The term used in referring to a fabric woven 27 inches in width (or ¾ of the standard yarn). It is a carryover from the early days of carpet weaving, when the European "ell" was the standard width for weaving carpet strips. Since an ell is equivalent to 27 inches and since the U.S. standard measure is the yard, the term ¾ carpet was coined.

Timing. The proper relationship of various actions and movements in the loom and the tufting machines.

Tip-Shearing. Texture pattern created in the same way as random-shearing, but generally less definite than random-sheared.

Tone on Tone. A carpet pattern made by using two or more shades of the same hue.

Top Colors. Colors of the yarn used to form the design, as distinguished from ground color.

Total Weight. Weight per square yarn of the total carpet pile, yarn, primary and secondary backings and coatings.

Traffic. The passing to and fro of persons with special reference to carpet wear resulting therefrom.

Tube Frames. A device on the Axminster loom consisting of a base member on which are mounted supports to receive pile yarn spools, guide tubes through which pile yarn ends are drawn, a friction device to provide tension while the spool is unrolling and catches to hold the assembly on an endless chain.

Tuft Bind. The force required to pull a tuft from a cut pile floor covering or to pull free one leg of a loop from a looped pile floor covering.

Tufted Carpet. Carpet or rug fabric that is not woven in the usual manner, but formed by the insertion of thousands of needles that punch tufts through a fabric backing on the principle of the sewing machine.

Tufting. Process of stitching fabric, leaving the stitches long enough to be cut off or left as loops.

Tufts. The cut loops of a pile fabric. Applies to both woven and tufted carpet.

Tunnel Test. A test method measuring flame spread, fuel contribution, and smoke density of building construction materials. Reference—ASTM E-84.

Twist Carpet. Surface texture created with tightly twisted yarns, resulting in a nubby or pebbly effect.

Twist Yarn. The number of turns about its axis per inch (TPI).

Two-Tone. A design or pattern obtained by using two shades of the same color.

Underlay. *See* Carpet Cushion.

Vat Dyes. Dyes formed in fabrics by oxidation and precipitation of the original dye liquor; e.g., indigo. Vat dyeing refers to a kind of dye rather than a method of dyeing. Raw stock dyeing, skein dyeing, or solution dyeing can be performed with vat dyes.

Velvet Carpet. A woven carpet made on a cam loom very similar to the Wilton loom, except that there is no Jacquard motion to control when each individual yarn rises to the surface. Today most velvet carpet produced is a level loop fabric in tweed or plain colors. Some cut pile plush or splush fabrics are also produced.

Velvet Finish. A term used to describe the surface of a dense cut pile carpet, produced usually on tufting machine or velvet loom. See also Plush, Splush, and Saxony Finish.

Vinyl. A synthetic carpet back which may be applied in either a ''hard'' or cushioned form.

Vinyl Foam Cushioning. A new kind of carpet cushioning made from a combination of solids and liquids. It is claimed that vinyl foam cushioning will not decompose.

Warp. A series of threads or yarns (usually delivered from a beam) running lengthwise in the carpet. Usually consists of chain, stuffer, and pile warp.

Warp Pile. An extra set of warp yarns woven into a fabric to form an up-right pile.

Waste. Fiber and yarn by-products created in the manufacturing and processing of fibers or yarns.

Weaving. Surface and backing yarns are interlaced, or woven together, in one operation. Several types of looms are employed. *See* Axminster, Wilton, Velvet.

Weft or Woof. The threads running across a woven fabric from selvage edge to selvage edge, binding in the pile and weaving in the warp threads.

Weighting. Finishing materials applied to a fabric to give increased weight.

Width. Distance between the two selvages of a cloth.

Wilton. Named after a town in England. This carpet weaving process employes a Jacquard pattern making mechanism, operating on the same principle as player piano rolls, with punched pattern cards determining pile height and color selection; most often used for patterns and multilevel textures.

Wire Height. The part on which the wires slide and wire hopper travels on a broad velvet or Wilton loom.

Wires. Metal strips inserted in the weaving shed in Wilton and velvet weaves so that the surface yarns are bound down over them, forming a loop of the proper height. In round wire constructions, loops are left uncut; in cut pile, flat wires with knife edges are used, cutting loops as wire is withdrawn.

Woolen Yarn. A rather soft, bulky yarn spun from both long and short wool fibers not combed out straight but lying in all directions so that they interlock and produce a felt-like texture.

Worsted Yarn. Made of long staple carpet fiber and combed to parallel the fiber and remove the extremely short fibers.

Woven Backing. Backing produced by a weaving process using natural fiber, such as jute, cotton duck synthetic yarns.

Yard Goods (Or Yardage). Cloth sold by the running yard as distinguished from made-up garments.

Yarn. A continuous strand for tufting, weaving, or knitting. (1) Continuous filament yarn: yarn formed into a continuous strand from two or more continuous filaments. (2) Spun yarn: yarn formed from staple by spinning or twisting into a single continuous strand or yarn.

Yarn Dyeing. Spun fiber or yarn dyed before carpet is manufactured.

Yarn Ply. The number of strands of single yarns twisted together to form one carpet yarn.

Yarn Size. Refer to Count.

Yarn Weight. Number of yards of yarn per unit of weight.

Bibliography

General Sources

"Basic Facts about the Carpet and Rug Industry" (pamphlet), American Carpet and Rug Institute, Inc., 1961, 1962, 1963, 1964.

"Cadon Contract Carpets N-11: A Treatise on Contract Carpet Made from Monsanto Anti-static BCF Nylon Carpet Yarns" (booklet), written and edited by F. C. Flindt, A.B., Monsanto Textiles Division, 1971.

"Carpet and Rugs" (booklet), a consumer publication from the General Services Administration, Federal Supply Service, 1972.

"Carpet and Rugs" (booklet), The Hoover Home Institute and Engineering Division, The Hoover Company, 1971.

The Carpet Specifiers' Handbook, 1974, The Carpet and Rug Institute, 1973.

The Economics of Carpeting and Resilient Flooring: An Evaluation and Comparison, by George M. Parks, Wharton School of Finance and Commerce, University of Pennsylvania, 1966.

Encyclopedia of Textiles, by the editors of *American Fabrics Magazine,* Prentice-Hall, Inc., 1972, 2nd ed.

"Man-Made Fiber Fact Book" (pamphlet), Man-Made Fiber Producers Association, Inc., 1972.

"Needlepunch Process," Technical Publications, Monsanto Textile Division, May 1967.

"The Selection and Maintenance of Commercial Carpets" (booklet), by Bernard Berkeley, American Hotel and Motel Association, 1970.

"Specifications Guide for Carpets of Antron/Education" (pamphlet), DuPont (undated).

"Specifications Guide for Carpet of Antron Nylon" (pamphlet), DuPont (undated).

"Standards for Commercial Carpet" (pamphlet: 4-GP-129), Canadian Government Specifications Board, Ottowa, Ontario.

Static Control

"Static Control in Carpets," by J. A. Gusack, *Modern Textiles Magazine,* January 1972.

Flammability

"Carpet Flammability" (staff article, with bibliography), *Building Operating Management,* November 1970.

"Of Carpets, Patient Safety, and Decision-Making at HEW," *Hospital Practice,* March 1971.

"Products to Improve Fire Safety for Manufacturers of Building and Construction Materials" (pamphlet), Monsanto Fire Safety Center, Bulletin MFSC-100 (undated).

"Report to the Surgical Forum" ("Results of Studies on the Biological Effects of Smoke from Carpet Fibers by Dr. Donald P. Dressler to the Annual Meeting of The American College of Physicians"), reported in *Medical World News,* Nov. 9, 1973.

"Report on a Test Method for Measuring the Flame Propagating Characteristics of Flooring and Floor Covering Materials" (booklet), File USNC-42, Underwriters Laboratories, 1970, rev. ed.

Maintenance

"Anso Contract Carpet Maintenance" (pamphlet), Fabrics Division, Allied Chemical Corporation (undated).

"Carpet Maintenance Manual" (pamphlet), Lee's Carpets, Division of Burlington Mills, 1972, rev. ed.

"How to Care for Your Carpets of Acrilan Plus Acrylic" (pamphlet), Monsanto (undated).

"How to Maintain Your Guaranteed Carpet of Anso Nylon" (pamphlet), Fibers Division, Allied Chemical (undated).

"Keep It Clean: An Extension Program for Contract Carpets" (pamphlet), Monsanto, 1972.

"Maintenance Housekeeping" (pamphlet), Cleaning Consultation Department, Monsanto (undated).

"Preventing Serious Carpet Problems," by Herbert Tracy, *The Executive Housekeeper*, August 1971.

Standards

Annual Book of ASTM Standards, American Society for Testing and Materials (revisions issued annually).

"Performance Certification: A Guide for Specifiers of Contract Carpet"

(pamphlet: G5), Dow-Badische, June 1972.

Technical Manual, American Association of Textile Chemists and Colorists (undated).

Hospitals

"Abstract: Effect of Newborn Nursery Carpeting on Environmental Microflora and the Bacterial Colonizing of Newborns," by Martin Keller, M.D., Ph.D.; R. Lanese, Ph.D.; C. R. MacPherson, M.D.; R. C. Covey, B.S., Ohio State University College of Medicine, Annual Meeting of the Public Health Association, Houston, Texas, 1970.

"Carpeting Found to Reduce Maintenance Costs 30%" (staff article), *The Nations Hospitals*, no. 4, 1969.

"Carpeting Increases Safety and Diminishes Apprehensiveness in the Child Patient" (staff article), *The Nations Hospitals*, no. 2, 1971.

"Carpeting the Ward: An Exploratory Study in Environmental Psychiatry," by Frances E. Cheek, Ph.D.; Robert Maxwell, Ph.D.; Richard Weisman, M.A., *Mental Hygiene,* vol. 55, no. 1 (January 1971).

"Hospital Carpet Flammability Standards: Confusion Reigns Supreme" (staff article), *Contract Magazine,* Mar. 19, 1972.

"Hospital Carpeting" (staff article), *Southern Hospitals,* May 1971.

"A 'Magic Carpet' for Newborns," by Thomas Pittman, *Hospital Forum,* May 1970.

"Microbiology of Hospital Carpeting," by James G. Shaffer, Sc.D., *Health Laboratory Science,* vol. 3, no. 2 (April 1966).

"Notes on the Meeting of the Havermeyer and Hospital Infections Committee," given by Edward Hedrick and Ernest E. Tucker, M.D., Chairman, Havermeyer and Hospital Infections Committee, Morristown Memorial Hospital, Morristown, N.J., Oct. 19, 1971.

"What Carpeting Must Do to Become Acceptable," by Frances Ginsberg, *Modern Hospitals,* April 1971.

Schools and Universities

"Carpeting and Learning" (report), by M. J. Conrad and N. L. Gibbons, Ohio State University, November 1963.

"Soft Floor Covering in the Los Angeles City School District" (report), by Donald D. Cunliff, May 1967.

Airports

"An Analysis of Carpet and Terrazzo for Use at San Francisco International Airport" (report), prepared by San Francisco Airport Architects, John Carl Warneke and Assoc./ Dryfuss and Blackford, Sept. 21, 1971.

"Report on Carpet Design for the Landside Building Tampa International Airport to Mr. George Bean, Hillsborough County Aviation Authority," by Joseph A. Maxwell and Assoc., Inc., June 1969.

Index